GLOBAL RECESSION – CAUSES, IMPACTS AND REMEDIES

RECESSION, DEPRESSION, AND UNEMPLOYMENT

GLOBAL RECESSION – CAUSES, IMPACTS AND REMEDIES

Additional books in this series can be found on Nova's website under the Series tab.

Additional E-books in this series can be found on Nova's website under the E-books tab.

ECONOMIC ISSUES, PROBLEMS AND PERSPECTIVES

Additional books in this series can be found on Nova's website under the Series tab.

Additional E-books in this series can be found on Nova's website under the E-books tab.

GLOBAL RECESSION – CAUSES, IMPACTS AND REMEDIES

RECESSION, DEPRESSION, AND UNEMPLOYMENT

DANIEL A. GARCÍA
EDITOR

Nova Science Publishers, Inc.
New York

For permission to use material from this book please contact us:
Telephone 631-231-7269; Fax 631-231-8175
Web Site: http://www.novapublishers.com

NOTICE TO THE READER

LIBRARY OF CONGRESSCATALOGING-IN-PUBLICATION DATA
Recession, depression, and unemployment / editor, Daniel A. Garcma.
p. cm.
Includes index.
ISBN 978-1-61761-508-5 (hbk.)
1. Unemployment--United States. 2. Recessions--United States. 3. Manpower policy--United States. 4. United States--Economic conditions--2009- 5. United States--Economic policy--2009- I. Garcma, Daniel A.
HD5724.R335 2010
331.13'70973--dc22
2010034020

Published by Nova Science Publishers, Inc. † New York

CONTENTS

PREFACE

The recession that began in the United States in December 2007 has been one of the deepest and longest since World War II. One feature that distinguishes the recent recession from its postwar predecessors is the historically high percentage of unemployed persons without jobs for more than six months (the long-term unemployed). This book explores the current global recession, and analyses the trend inn long-term unemployment with considerations to policymakers to enact legislation to stimulate job growth and provide additional benefits to unemployment workers and their families.

Chapter 1- The recession that began in the United States in December 2007 has been one of the deepest and longest since World War II. One feature that distinguishes the recent recession from its postwar predecessors is the historically high percentage of unemployed persons without jobs for more than six months (the long-term unemployed). This chapter analyzes the trend in long-term unemployment over the postwar period and offers explanations for its unusually high incidence during the most recent postwar recession. It compares the individual, job, and household characteristics of the long-term unemployed during the latest recession (2007-2009) with the long-term unemployed at the end of the two previous recessions (1990-1991 and 2001).

Chapter 2- After the long economic expansion that characterized much of the current decade, the nation entered its 11th postwar recession in December 2007. The subsequent decrease in jobs and comparison of the latest recession to the Great Depression intensified congressional interest in passing legislation early in 2009 aimed at encouraging creation of new jobs and warding off further loss of jobs.

To mitigate all but one recession since the 1960s, Congress chose to increase federal spending on public works (infrastructure). (See CRS Report

92-93 9, *Countercyclical Job Creation Programs.*) Public works expenditures traditionally have gone to certain types of construction activities (e.g., building highways and bridges, dams and flood control structures) which indirectly increase demand in industries that supply their products to construction firms (e.g., manufacturing). Today, the definition of infrastructure has been expanded to include green economic activities (commonly referred to as green jobs), which include industries that utilize renewable resources (e.g., electricity generated by wind), produce energy-efficient goods and services (e.g., mass transit), and install energy-conserving products (e.g., retrofitting buildings with thermal-pane windows).

Chapter 3- The economy has been showing signs that the worst of the recession that began in December 2007 may be over.[1] But, one economic indicator that is very visible in people's daily lives—the unemployment rate—continues to rise. With the unemployment rate at 9.7% in August 2009,[2] those still employed or able to find jobs 20 months into the recession are quite likely to know personally others who have been less fortunate. In addition, the still high and rising percentage of workers without jobs for so long that their eligibility for unemployment benefits soon might be exhausted[3] is of concern to Members of Congress who have extended benefit duration on more than one occasion since the recession's onset.[4] And, there is consternation in some quarters that firms thus far have not begun to hire or recall from layoff more workers than leave their employ despite enactment in February 2009 of the American Recovery and Reinvestment Act (P.L. 111-5).

Chapter 4- This chapter describes the history of temporary federal extensions to unemployment benefits from 1980 to the present. Among these extensions is the Emergency Unemployment Compensation (EUC08) program created by P.L. 110-252 (amended by P.L. 110-449 and P.L. 111-5). It also provides information on the legislative timing of those temporary programs. Additionally, the report includes information on economic recessions and possible triggers for the extension of unemployment benefits.

This chapter contains four sections. The first section provides background information on unemployment compensation (UC) benefits. It also provides a brief summary of UC benefit exhaustion and how exhaustion rates are related to the business cycle.

The second section provides the definition of a recession as well as the determination process for declaring a recession. It also provides information on the timing of all recessions since 1980.

Chapter 5- A good deal of commentary has addressed similarities between the recession that began in December 2007 and the Great Depression.

Comparisons between the two have extended beyond conditions in financial markets to conditions in the labor market. The analogy appears to be fueled by projections that the unemployment rate could reach double digits in the coming months.

Little if any comparative labor market research has been undertaken, however. To address the situation, this chapter analyzes the experiences of workers during the 1930s, which encompassed the almost five years of the Great Depression. Because it was a period very distant and different from today, the report devotes considerable time to examining the employment and unemployment measures then available. The report ends by comparing the labor market conditions of the 1930s with those encountered by workers thus far during the nation's eleventh recession of the post-World War II period.

Chapter 6- With the exception of the Great Depression, the recession that began in December 2007 is the nation's most severe according to various labor market indicators. The 7.1 million jobs cut from employer payrolls between December 2007 and September 2009, when it is thought the latest recession might have ended, is more than has been recorded for any postwar recession. Job loss was greater in a relative sense during the latest recession as well, recording a 5.1% decrease over the period.[1] In addition, long-term unemployment (defined as the proportion of workers without jobs for longer than 26 weeks) was higher in September 2009—at 36%—than at any time since 1948.[2]

Chapter 7- According to the National Bureau of Economic Research (NBER), the U.S. economy entered a recession in December 2007. It is now the longest recession of the post-World War II era. The recession can be separated into two distinct phases. During the first phase, which lasted for the first half of 2008, the recession was not deep as measured by the decline in gross domestic product (GDP) or the rise in unemployment. It then deepened from the third quarter of 2008 to the first quarter of 2009. The economy continued to contract slightly in the second quarter of 2009, before beginning to grow in the third quarter. This recession features the largest decline in output, consumption, and investment, and the largest increase in unemployment, of any post-war recession.

Chapter 8- The National Bureau of Economic Research (NBER) recently announced that the economy had reached a cyclical peak and that a recession had begun in December 2007. A recession is one of several discrete phases in the overall business cycle. The term may often be used loosely to describe an economy that is slowing down or characterized by weakness in at least one major sector like the housing market. When used by economists, "recession" means a significant decline in overall economic activity that lasts more than a few months. NBER business cycle dating committee is the generally recognized arbiter of the dates of the beginnings and ends of recessions. With all statistics it takes some time to compile the data, which means they are only available after the events they describe. Moreover, because it takes time to discern changes in trends given the usual month-to-month volatility in economic indicators, and because the data are subject to revision, it takes some time before the dating committee can agree that a recession began at a certain date. It can be a year or more after the fact that the dating committee announces the date of the beginning of a recession. Just as it took some time for the business cycle dating committee to determine when the recession began, it is likely to be some time after the fact that they determine when the recession has come to an end.

Chapter 9- Each year, even when the economy is growing, millions of people lose a job for reasons other than poor performance or misconduct. The ability of employers to quickly adjust the size of their workforces in response to changes in demand is generally considered a source of strength for the U.S. economy over the long term, because it prompts a shift of labor resources toward areas of higher productivity. Some people, however, bear substantial costs from employers' flexibility—particularly during recessions, when many people lose jobs and new opportunities are relatively scarce.

This issue brief reviews the research on the short- and long-term effects of involuntary job loss for reasons other than poor performance or misconduct on people's future employment and earnings.[1] In light of the recession that began in December 2007 and the Congressional Budget Office's (CBO's) projection that, under current law, the unemployment rate will remain elevated for a number of years, the brief focuses on the effects of involuntary job loss during periods of weak economic activity.[2] The brief also summarizes some of the government programs that help people who have lost their job.

In: Recession, Depression, and Unemployment ISBN: 978-1-61761-508-5
Editors: Daniel A. García

Chapter 1

LONG-TERM UNEMPLOYMENT AND RECESSIONS

Gerald Mayer and Linda Levine

SUMMARY

The recession that began in the United States in December 2007 has been one of the deepest and longest since World War II. One feature that distinguishes the recent recession from its postwar predecessors is the historically high percentage of unemployed persons without jobs for more than six months (the long-term unemployed). This chapter analyzes the trend in long-term unemployment over the postwar period and offers explanations for its unusually high incidence during the most recent postwar recession. It compares the individual, job, and household characteristics of the long-term unemployed during the latest recession (2007-2009) with the long-term unemployed at the end of the two previous recessions (1990-1991 and 2001).

Long-term unemployment varies across individuals based on demographic and job characteristics. In each of the last three recessions, older unemployed workers were more likely than younger workers to have been unemployed for over six months. While an equal share of unemployed men and women were unemployed for over half a year during the last two recessions, unemployed women were less likely than men to have been out of work for 27 or more weeks at the end of the 1990-1991 recession. Unlike the two previous recessions, in 2009, unemployed workers with less than a high school education were more likely than unemployed workers with more education to have been out of work for at least six months. Also in 2009, workers laid off from the financial activities and information industries were the most likely to have been jobless longer than 26 weeks. Workers displaced from management, business, and financial occupations were most at risk of long-term unemployment during recent recessions.

Unemployment affects both the individuals who are without work and their families. Households of the long-term unemployed have lower earnings and income than other households (where households include married couples, single parents, and single individuals). In 2008, the most recent year for which data are available, the long-term unemployed were more likely than all unemployed workers to live in households with incomes below the official poverty line. They were more likely than other unemployed workers to receive benefits from the Supplemental Nutrition Assistance Program (SNAP, formerly the Food Stamp program) or be covered by Medicaid. In 2008, only 2.7% of the long-term unemployed received public assistance.

Slightly over half (5 5%) of the long-term unemployed had some type of health insurance coverage at some time during 2008, compared to a larger majority (84%) of employed workers. Although a small majority (5 8%) of the long-term unemployed were homeowners in 2008, they were less likely than employed workers (72%) to own their own homes.

As the economy recovers and employers increase hiring to meet the growing demand for goods and services, many currently unemployed workers will be able to find new jobs. However, finding work may be more difficult for the long-term unemployed if, for example, employers think their skills have deteriorated during their lengthy time away from the workplace. The longterm unemployed displaced from industries in which restructuring has occurred may also have a hard time finding new jobs in other industries, especially if the jobs require skills different from those they possess. Policies to encourage employers to hire the long-term unemployed include wage and training subsidies. Offering wage insurance and reemployment bonuses to unemployed workers may encourage them to accept jobs sooner than they otherwise might have.

The recession that began in the United States in December 2007 has been one of the deepest and longest since World War II. In response, Congress enacted legislation to stimulate aggregate demand and provide assistance to unemployed workers and their families. The American Recovery and Reinvestment Act of 2009 (ARRA, P.L. 111-5) temporarily raised spending by increasing funding for a number of programs, creating new programs, and providing tax benefits for individuals, families and businesses. Congress also authorized a federally funded temporary program (P.L. 110-252 as amended) to provide additional weeks of unemployment benefits to those who exhausted their eligibility under the federal-state Unemployment Compensation (UC) program. Although some in the public policy community are concerned that extending benefits may discourage recipients from looking for work,[1] Congress has extended the program on multiple occasions.[2]

It is not unusual for improvement in the labor market, as measured by a declining unemployment rate, to begin some months after the official ending date of a recession.[3] It is also not unusual for the proportion of the labor force unemployed for more than six months (the long-term unemployment rate) to continue rising and peak after a recession's end. What is unusual, however, is that the incidence of long-term unemployment currently is higher than at any time in the postwar period.

The purpose of this chapter is to assist policymakers who may consider legislation to stimulate job growth, provide additional benefits to unemployed workers, or assist families whose incomes have fallen because of a job loss or reduction in hours worked. The report first compares the prevalence of long-term unemployment across business cycles during the postwar period and offers explanations for its unusually high incidence during the most recent postwar recession. It next analyzes the likelihood of unemployed workers with different demographic, job, and household characteristics experiencing a very long period without paychecks. The report closes with a discussion of long-term unemployment's implications for public policy.

THE TREND IN LONG-TERMUNEMPLOYMENT

The percentage of the labor force without jobs for longer than six months (the long-term unemployment rate)—like the unemployment rate—generally rises as economic activity falls. This countercyclical pattern was evident during the deep recessions of the 1 970s and 1 980s, when the long-term unemployment rate rose 0.4 percentage points to 0.8% at the 1973-1975 recession's end and 1.1 percentage points to 2.1% at the 198 1-1982 recession's end.[4] The same pattern was evident during milder recessions, when the long-term unemployment rate rose 0.3 percentage points to 0.8% at the trough of the 1990-1991 and 2001 recessions. As the latest recession unfolded, the long-term unemployment rate increased from 0.9% in December 2007 to 3.3% inAugust 2009 (the recession's ending date used in this chapter).5 Not only was this 2.4 percentage point increase much greater than recorded during prior recessions, but it also put the long-term unemployment rate at a postwar high. (See Figure 1.)

As also shown in Figure 1, the long-term unemployment rate continues to rise during the early stage of recoveries. For example, the share of the labor force without jobs for more than six months increased from 3.3% in August 2009 to 4.1% in January 2010. The rate rose further to 4.3% in March, the latest month for which data from the Current Population Survey (CPS) are available from the U.S. Bureau of Labor Statistics (BLS).

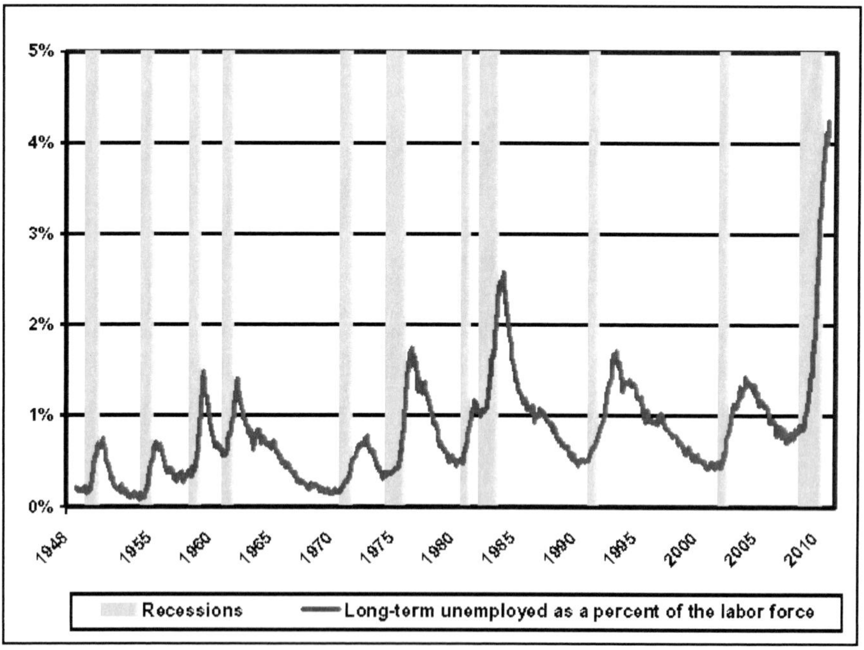

Source: CRS analysis of data from the Current Population Survey (CPS).

Figure 1. Long-Term Unemployed as a Percentage of the Labor Force,1948 to 2010, Seasonally Adjusted.

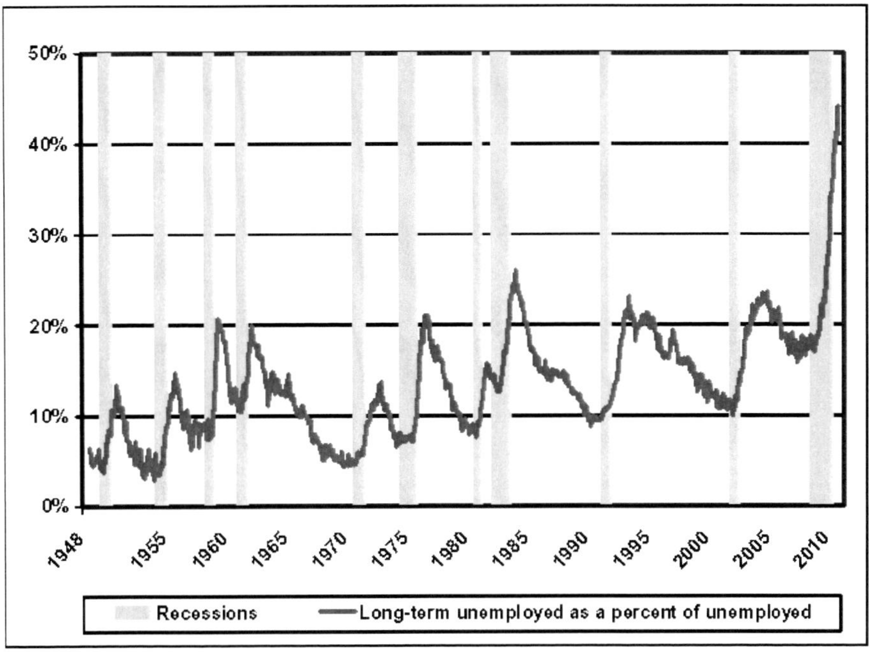

Source: Bureau of Labor Statistics (BLS) data from the Current Population Survey (CPS).

Figure 2. Long-Term Unemployed as a Percentage of Unemployed Workers, 1948 to 2010, Seasonally Adjusted.

Another way to look at the trend in long-term unemployment is as a proportion of total unemployment. The long-term unemployed's share of all unemployed individuals was 33.6% in August 2009, up from 17.3% in December 2007.[6] This measure also continues to rise during the early stage of recoveries. It rose to 44.1% in March 2010, as fewer people flowed into (short-term) unemployment. The proportion of unemployed persons out-of-work over 26 weeks has been considerably above the rate recorded during prior downturns and nascent recoveries. (See Figure 2.)

WHY SO HIGH DURING THE LATESTRECESSION ANDNASCENTRECOVERY?

The historically high incidence of long-term unemployment observed starting in mid-2009[7] coincides with Congress' lengthier than usual temporary extension of UC benefits beyond the duration afforded by the permanently authorized federal-state UC system and Extended Benefit programs.[8] The shorter-lived temporary UC benefit programs enacted to mitigate the effects ofseven prior recessions provided a maximum of 13 to 33 weeks of benefits. After the seven recessions ended, the long-term unemployment rate and share of long-term unemployment ranged from 0.8% to 2.6% and from 13.6% to 25.7%, respectively.[9] The 111th Congress provided a maximum of 33 weeks of benefits from about November 2008 through October 2009. Both the long-term unemployment rate (3.7%) and the share of long-term unemployment (36.0%) in October 2009 were well outside these ranges. The subsequent extension of benefits to amaximum of 53 weeks starting in November 2009 has been accompanied by a still higher longterm unemployment rate and share of long-term unemployment in early 2010. (See Figure 1 and Figure 2.)

The availability of a maximum of 53 weeks of benefits through the Emergency Unemployment Compensation (EUC) program probably has prompted individuals to continue searching for jobs instead of leaving the labor force due to discouragement over their job prospects upon exhausting their regular UC benefits.[10] But, the currently low hiring rate of employers makes workers refraining from accepting jobs in order to continue receiving EUC benefits a less plausible explanation for the historically high incidence of long-term unemployment. An analysis by Valletta and Kuang that estimated the difference in duration of unemployment among persons likely to be eligible for UC benefits (i.e., job losers) and those likely to be ineligible (i.e., unemployed job leavers and labor force entrants) similarly concluded that the recent extensions of unemployment benefits contributed little to the historically high prevalence of long-term unemployment. "It is not surprising that the disincentive effects of UI would loom small in the midst of the most severe labor market downturn since the Great Depression."[11]According to BLS data from the Job Openings and Labor Turnover Survey, for example, the hiring rate fell from 3.6% in December 2007 to 3.1% in August 2009. It remained largely unchanged throughFebruary 2010, the latest month for which data are available. In contrast, the hiring rate duringthe March-November 2001 recession and ensuing "jobless recovery" exceeded the hiring rate reported during and after the 2007-2009 recession. The hiring rate fell from 4.4% in March 2001 to 3.9% in November 2001, after which it reached a low of 3.5% in March 2003 before gradually trending upward. [12]

The greater industry restructuring that arguably characterized the 2001 recession may have coincided with the latest recession as well, and made it more difficult for workers to find new jobs as quickly as they did after earlier recessions. Workers displaced by industries permanently reducing their demand for labor will take longer to become reemployed than workers waiting to be recalled by their employers from temporary layoffs. The period of job search could be especially prolonged when the skill sets needed for employment in growing industries differ from the skills sets of workers laid off by restructuring industries and when displaced workers must substantially lower their wage expectations to obtain new jobs.[13]

The so-called jobless recovery from the 2001 recession prompted several economists to analyze whether increased industry restructuring had led comparatively large numbers of unemployed workers to move from downsizing industries to industries increasing their demand for labor. No consensus was reached, however. Groshen and Potter estimated that, according to their measure, many more industries were undergoing restructuring during the 2001 recession and subsequent recovery than during prior business cycles.[14] In contrast, Aaronson, Rissman, and Sullivan estimated that, based on a different measure of labor reallocation across industries, the degree of restructuring during and after the 2001 recession was less than that during earlier periods. Although this second group of researchers did not find evidence that the rate of permanent job loss was atypically elevated following the 2001 recession, they noted that "the unusually high duration of unemployment [in 2002 and 2003] is consistent with [an] increased mismatch" between the skills of displaced workers and the skills being demanded by employers in growing industries.[15] Similarly, Figura and Wascher estimated that workers displaced from downsizing industries experienced almost a doubling in their time spent not working (from 19 to 35 weeks) between the 1997-1999 and 2001-2003 periods, while workers displaced from other industries exhibited a much smaller increase (from 19 to 28 weeks). The two researchers concluded that while it appears downsizing industries (e.g., manufacturing, information and data processing services, broadcasting and telecommunications, publishing) were quick to layoff workers in the early 2000s, "it took a considerable amount of time for these resources to be re-employed elsewhere."[16]

Rissman's more recent work, covering the period from the first quarter of 1984 to the second quarter of 2009, suggests that the impact of structural realignment on unemployed workers varies by industry. While restructuring in the finance, insurance, and real estate industries resulted in worker displacement, employees from these industries may be "better able to find alternativeemployment in other sectors of the economy because the skills they possess are more readily transferable to employment in other industries."

Alternatively, workers who lose jobs in the construction, manufacturing, and transportation and utilities industries "may be less readily absorbed into other sectors," thereby lengthening the time spent unemployed.[17]

Distinguishing cyclical from structural unemployment is more than an academic exercise. If job losses are the result of a temporary (cyclical) reduction in the demand for goods and services, the use of fiscal and monetary policies to stimulate economic activity is appropriate. However, if job losses also result from changes in technology, trade, or consumer taste that prompt permanent shifts in the demand for labor across sectors, then employment policies are suitable measures to enact as well. This matter will be revisited in "Implications for Public Policy" at the conclusion of this chapter.

WHOISLIKELY TO EXPERIENCE LONG-TERMUNEMPLOYMENT?

Knowledge of which jobless workers are more likely to suffer very long spells of unemployment may help to identify policies that address their plight. This chapter compares the long-term unemployed at the end of the three most recent recessions (2007-2009, 2001, and 1990-1991). The report uses data from the monthly Current Population Survey (CPS), which is a household survey conducted by the U.S. Census Bureau for BLS. The report also uses data from the Annual Social and Economic (ASEC) Supplement to the CPS. The supplement collects information on the sources and amounts of household and family income and benefits. (The ASEC Supplement was formerly called the March Supplement.) [18]

Because of changes in the CPS over time, not all variables analyzed in this chaptercan be compared across the last three recessions. For example, beginning in January 2003, the CPS adopted new industry and occupation classification systems that substantially changed the way in which some industries and occupations are categorized. In January 2003, the CPS also changed the way survey respondents can respond to the question on race. While in the past survey respondents had to select one race (e.g., white, black), respondents can now pick more than one race, which makes meaningful comparisons over time difficult. Finally, because the CPS is a household survey, the size of some cells (e.g., number of workers with an advanced or professional degree) limits the detail of the analysis presented below.

Individual Characteristics

Age

Age appears to be positively related to long-term unemployment. As shown in Figure 3, older unemployed workers are more likely to have been without jobs for longer than half a year in 2009, 2001, and 1991. In 2009, for example, 30.4% of unemployed 25-34 year olds and 33.1% of unemployed 3 5-44 year olds had been out of work for at least 27 weeks, compared to 3 7.5% of unemployed 45-54 year olds, 39.2% of unemployed 55-64 year olds, and 40.0% of unemployed workers age 65 and older.

Age (a proxy for seniority) tends to protect older workers from being laid off and thereby contributes to the comparatively lower unemployment rate of older workers. But, seniority affords older workers little protection if companies go out of business or close plants. Once they are let go, the higher earnings that often accompany more job tenure would tend to lead older workers to remain unemployed longer than younger workers. Joblessness could be especially prolonged among high-wage, high-tenure persons displaced from industries undergoing structural change in addition to temporarily reduced product demand (e.g., workers in the motor vehicle manufacturing industry).[19]

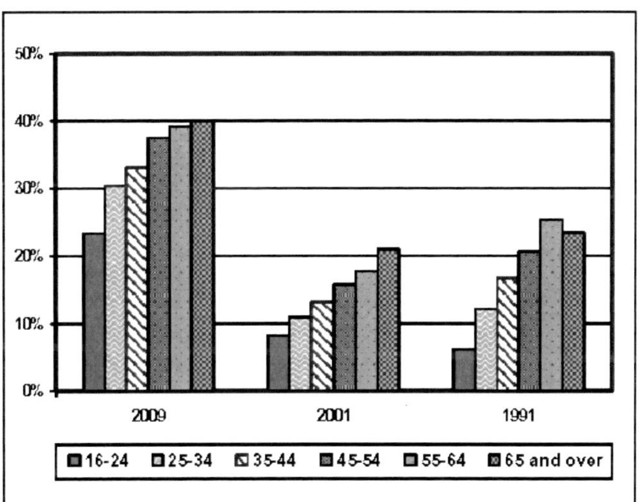

Source: CRS analysis of data from the Current Population Survey (CPS).

Figure 3. Percentage of Unemployed by Age Group Who are Long-Term Unemployed, 2009, 2001 , and 1991.

Gender

Unemployment among men has been greater than among women during and shortly after recessions since the 1980 recession. The latest recession is no exception, with men's higher unemployment rate related in part to their dominance of employment in more cyclically sensitive industries (e.g., manufacturing and construction).[20]

A notable change across recent recessions involves the likelihood of long-term unemployment by gender. Figure 4 shows that in 2009 and 2001, unemployed women were as likely as unemployed men to be out-of-work for over half a year. In 1991, in contrast, unemployed women were significantly less likely than men to experience long-term joblessness.[21]The gap between their probability of long-term unemployment narrowed from 4.8 percentage points in favor of men in 1991 to a statistically insignificant 0.5 percentage points in 2001 and 2009. Women's increased attachment to the labor force may partly explain their labor market behavior becoming more like that of men: rather than immediately withdrawing from the workforce upon being laid off,women have become more likely to seek new jobs and to persist in their job search for a very long time.[22]

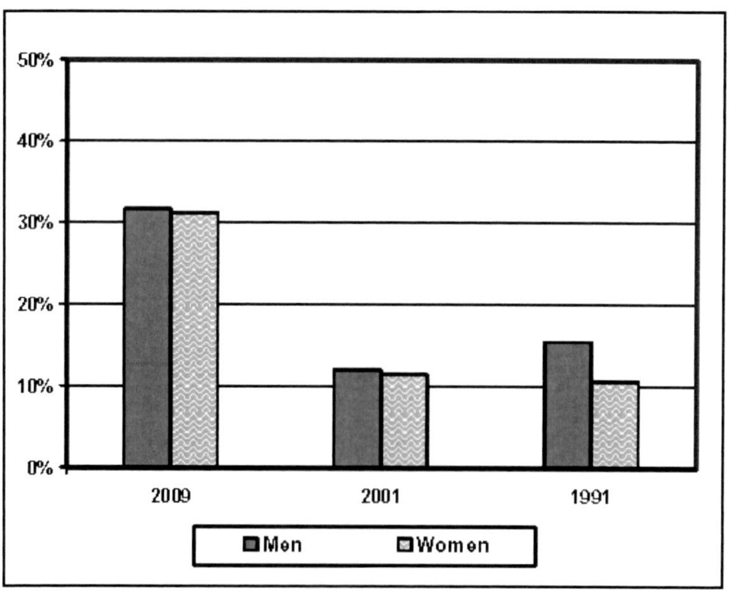

Source: CRS analysis of data from the Current Population Survey (CPS).

Figure 4. Percentage of Unemployed by Gender Who are Long-Term Unemployed, 2009, 2001 , and 1991.

EducationalAttainment

Another notable change concerns the probability of long-term unemployment among the unemployed who ended their formal schooling upon attainment of a high school diploma. They were more likely to be without jobs for longer than 26 weeks in 2009, while their risk of long-term unemployment did not differ substantially from that of other educational groups in 2001 and 1991. (See Figure 5.) In part, this change may have occurred because major employers of high school graduates age 25 and older were harder hit during this recession than during the two prior recessions. In 2009, the construction (10.8%) and manufacturing (13.6%) industries employed almost one-fourth of high school graduates in the labor force.[23] Construction employment plummeted by 21.4% between December 2007 and August 2009, compared to only 1.1% during the 2001 recession and 7.5% during the 1990-1991 recession.[24] Similarly, manufacturing employment dropped by 14.9% during the latest recession compared to only 6.6% during the 2001 recession and 3.2% during the 1990-1991 recession.

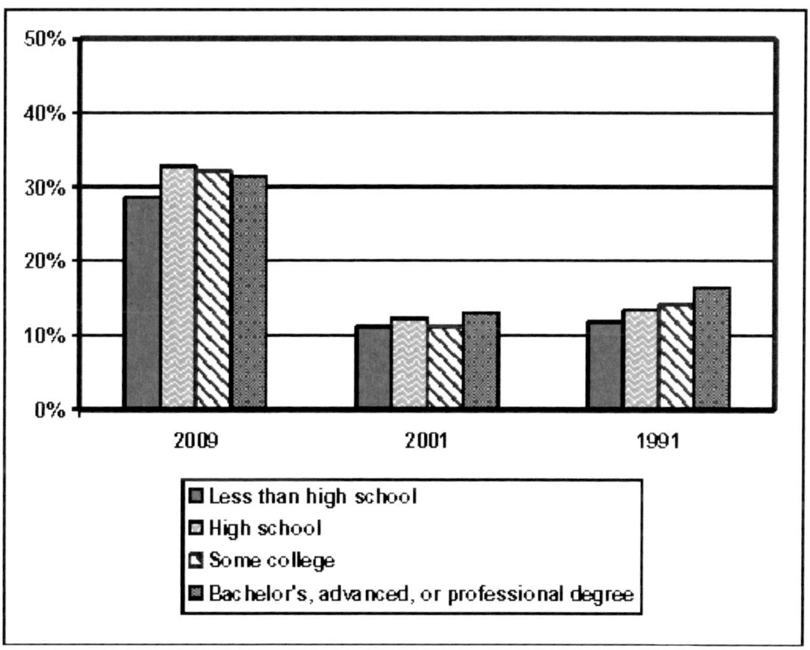

Source: CRS analysis of data from the Current Population Survey (CPS).

Figure 5. Percentage of Unemployed by Education Who are Long-TermUnemployed, 2009, 2001 , and 1991.

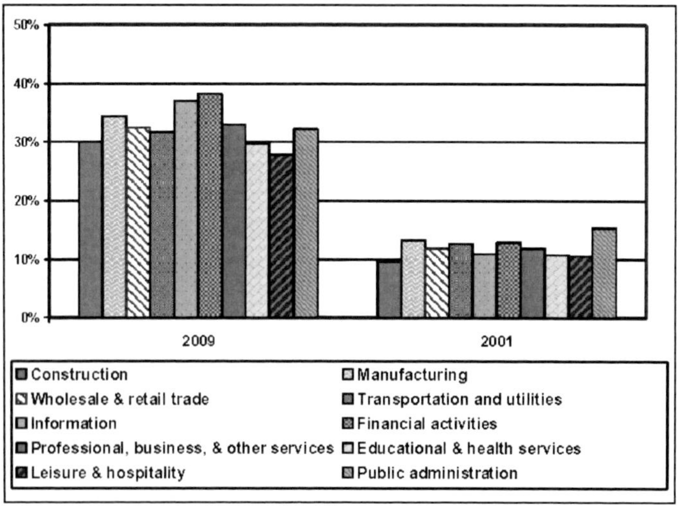

Source: CRS analysis of data from the Current Population Survey (CPS).

Note: This chart does not include mining or agriculture. In 2009, each of these industries accounted for less than 2% of total employment.

Figure 6. Percentage of Unemployed by Industry Who are Long-Term Unemployed, 2009 and 2001.

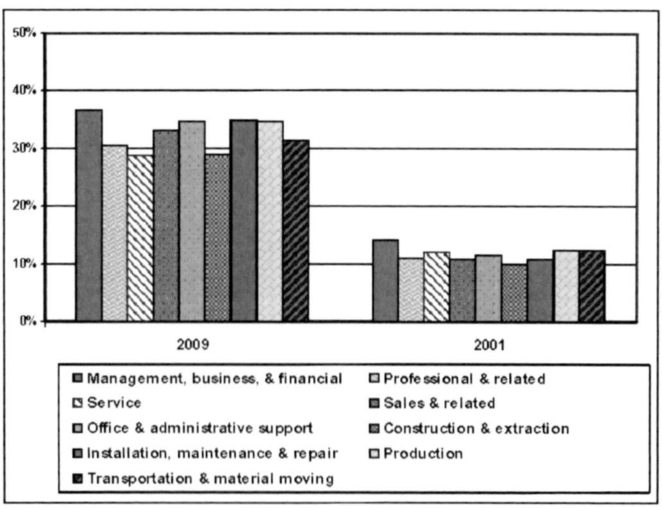

Source: CRS analysis of data from the Current Population Survey (CPS).

Note: This chart does not include farming occupations.

Figure 7. Percentage of Unemployed by Occupation Who are Long-Term Unemployed, 2009 and 2001.

Industry

Seemingly unique to this recession is the significantly greater risk of long-term unemployment among workers laid off from the information (e.g., telecommunications, publishing) and financial activities (i.e., finance, insurance, and real estate) industries. Almost two out of five workers laid off from the two industries did not receive a paycheck for over six months in 2009. In fact, long-term unemployment accounted for a larger percentage of total unemployment in the two industries than it did in the cyclically sensitive manufacturing industry (at a little more than one- third). Nonetheless, displaced manufacturing workers consistently were among the industries most likely to experience long-term unemployment. (See Figure 6.)

Occupation

Both in 2009 and 2001, workers displaced from management, business, and financial occupations had a greater probability of being unemployed for more than six months compared to workers laid off from other occupations. The relatively high wages of individuals in management, business, and financial occupations probably contributed to their lengthy unemployment while searching for jobs offering comparable compensation. So, too, would their industry-specific (not- easily transferable) skills if they needed to change industries to obtain new jobs. In contrast, only in 2009 were workers laid off from office and administrative support jobs significantly more likely to experience long-term unemployment. The overrepresentation of office and administrative support workers in two industries (information and financial activities) hit uncharacteristically hard during the 2007-2009 recession might have contributed to the occupational group's elevated risk of long-term unemployment.25 (See Figure 7.)

Household Characteristics

Unemployment affects both the individuals who are without work and their families. Workers who become unemployed face a loss of earnings and, in some cases, fringe benefits, such as employer contributions for health insurance or to a retirement plan. As a result, their families may experience a loss of household income and health insurance coverage. Unemployed homeowners may find it difficult to keep up with their mortgage payments and could face foreclosure.

At the same time, workers who become unemployed may be eligible for UC benefits, food assistance, or cash public assistance. Under the Consolidated Omnibus Budget Reconciliation Actof 1985 (COBRA, P.L. 99-272), they may be able to purchase health insurance through their former employer. Workers could be eligible for a temporary subsidy to buy health insurance under COBRA. Some workers may be eligible for a health coverage income tax credit (HCTC). Unemployed workers may also be covered by the insurance policy of another family member or they may be eligible for Medicaid.

This section compares workers who have been unemployed for 27 weeks or more with all unemployed workers and all employed workers. The analysis compares "all households" with married couple households. All types of households includes married couples, single parent households, and single individuals.

The analysis in this section is based on data from the Annual Social and Economic (ASEC) Supplement to the monthly CPS. The supplement collects information on household earnings and income for the previous year. The supplement also asks individuals whether they had health insurance at any time during the previous year. The supplement is conducted at the beginning of each year, mainly in March. The most recent data available are for 2008.

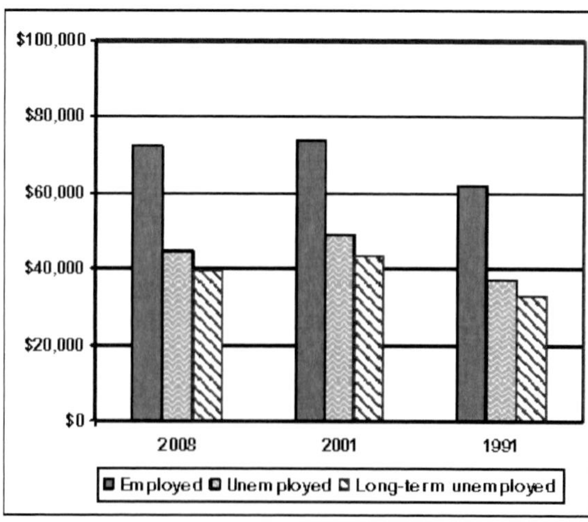

Source: CRS analysis of data from the Annual Social and Economic (ASEC) Supplement to the Current Population Survey (CPS).

Figure 8. Average Annual Real Earnings, All Households, 2008, 2001, and 1991(in 2009 dollars).

The data from the CPS supplement have some limitations in analyzing the household characteristics of workers unemployed for more than six months. Since the supplement collects information for the previous year (when a long-term unemployed worker may have been employed), it may not fully capture the household characteristics of workers at the time the survey is conducted.

In household surveys like the CPS, households tend to under report their income. Households report their wages and salaries more accurately than their income from interest, dividends, public assistance, or other sources. [26] Thus, the estimates in this section may understate the percentage of individuals or households receiving different types of income or benefits.

Earnings and Income

Figure 8 shows the average real earnings of households in 2008, 2001, and 1991. Average earnings are shown for employed workers, unemployed workers, and long-term unemployed workers. Unemployed workers include both the long-term unemployed and other unemployed persons. Average earnings are in constant (i.e., inflation-adjusted) 2009 dollars.

In 2008, the average household earnings of workers unemployed for more than six months were lower than the average household earnings of employed workers. The long-term unemployed had average household earnings that were about 55% of the average household earnings of employed workers ($39,780 compared to $72,450). The difference in average household earnings between the long-term unemployed and employed workers was similar in both 2001 and 1991.

Households may have income from sources other than work. For example, they may receive rent, interest, or dividends, as well as cash income in the form of UC benefits or public assistance. In 2008, the average household income of long-term unemployed workers was approximately $43,390. Again, this was about 55% of the average household income of employed workers ($78,350), and similar to the patterns in 2001 and 1991. (See Figure 9.)

Married couples have higher average earnings than all household types considered together. In 2008, as shown in Figure 10, married couples with at least one spouse unemployed for over six months had average earnings of $60,210 (compared to $39,780 for all household types). The average earnings of married couples with at least one long-term unemployed spouse were approximately three-fifths (61%) of the average earnings of married couples in which neither spouse was unemployed ($60,210 compared to $98,440). This percentage was slightly lower than in 2001 (64%), but higher than in 1991 (54%).

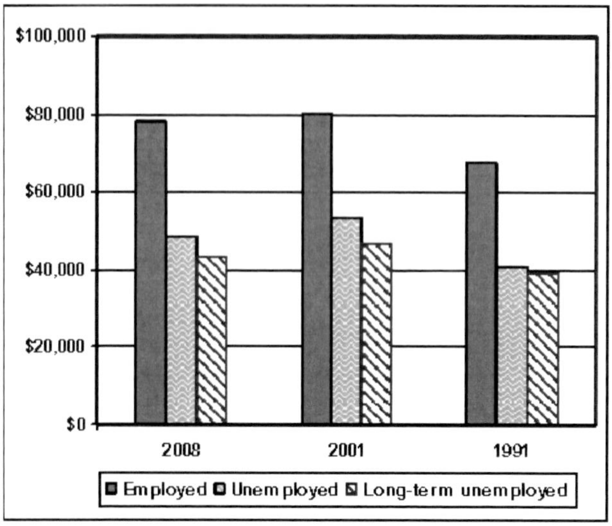

Source: CRS analysis of data from the Annual Social and Economic (ASEC) Supplement to the Current Population Survey (CPS).

Figure 9. Average Annual Real Income, All Households, 2008, 2001, and 1991 (in 2009 dollars).

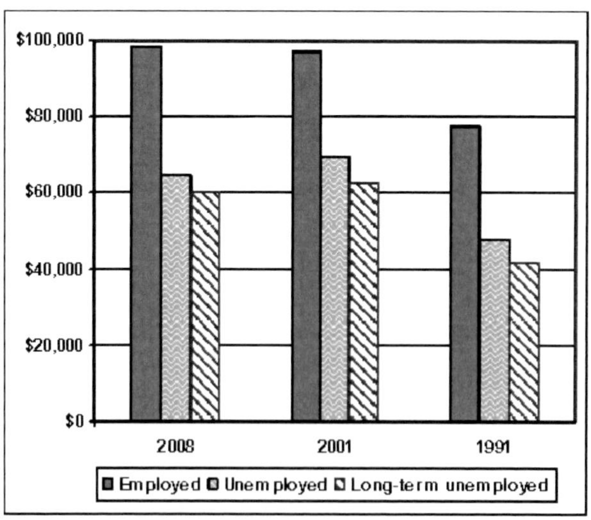

Source: CRS analysis of data from the Annual Social and Economic (ASEC) Supplement to the Current Population Survey (CPS).

Figure 10. Average Annual Real Earnings, Married Couples, 2008, 2001, and 1991 (in 2009 dollars).

The average income of married couples is higher than their average earnings. Figure 11 shows that in 2008, the average income of married couples with at least one long-term unemployed spouse was $70,370, which was about two-thirds of the average income of married couples with no unemployed spouse ($106,130). This was the same percentage as in 2001, but higher than in 1991 (61%).

UnemploymentBenefits

In 2008, almost a third (31.7%) of long-term unemployed workers received unemployment benefits (e.g., UC, EB and EUC benefits, Trade Adjustment Assistance).[27] As shown in Table 1, this was the same as in 2001 (30.6%), but lower than in 1991 (48.5%).[28]

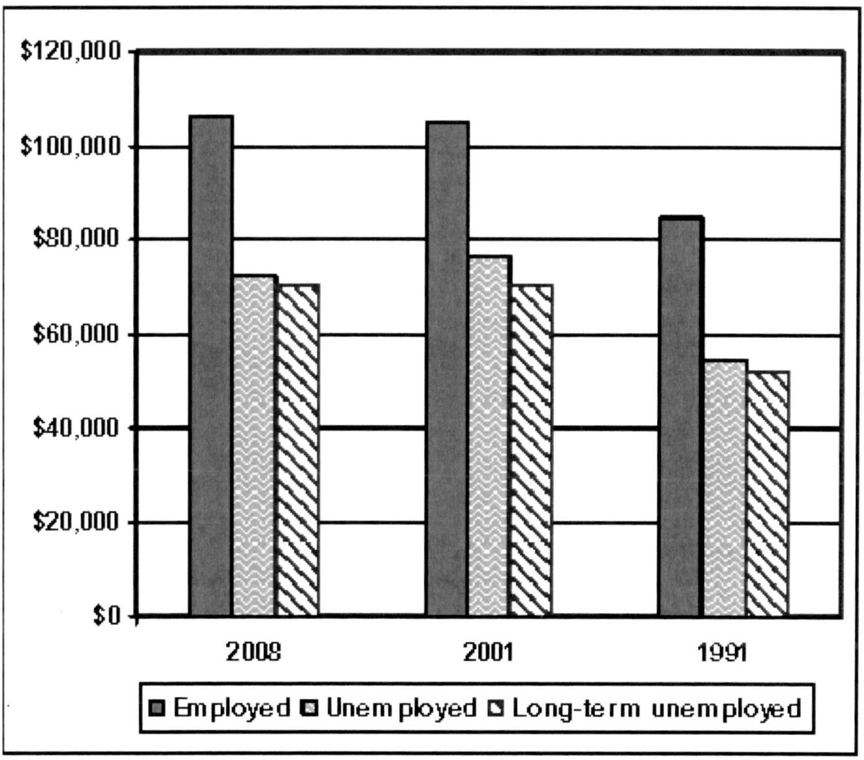

Source: CRS analysis of data from the Annual Social and Economic (ASEC) Supplement to the Current Population Survey (CPS).

Figure 11. Average Annual Real Income, Married Couples, 2008, 2001, and 1991 (in 2009 dollars).

Table 1. Percent of Employed, Unemployed, and Long-Term Unemployed byIndividual or Household Characteristic, 2008, 2001, and 1991

Characteristic	Labor Force Status of Individual	2008	2001	1991
Individual received unemployment compensation	Employed	2.8	3.5	5.0
	All unemployed	23.5	22.0	29.9
	Long-term unemployed[a]	31.7	30.6	48.5
Individual lived in a household below poverty	Employed	6.3	5.8	6.3
	All unemployed	21.0	20.5	23.5
	Long-term unemployed	31.0	27.1	27.4
Someone in the household received benefits under the Supplemental Nutrition Assistance Program (SNAP, formerly the Food Stamp program)	Employed	4.1	2.6	3.8
	All unemployed	15.7	13.1	18.0
	Long-term unemployed	20.3	15.7	19.3
Individual was covered by Medicaid	Employed	4.3	3.1	2.3
	All unemployed	12.1	11.1	11.9
	Long-term unemployed	15.5	12.8	11.1
Individual received public assistance[b]	Employed	0.3	0.4	0.9
	All unemployed	2.0	3.0	7.7
	Long-term unemployed	2.7	4.3	7.6

Source: CRS analysis of data from the Annual Social and Economic (ASEC) Supplement to the Current Population Survey (CPS).

Note: The unit of analysis is either the individual or the household. Thus, in 2008, 2.8% of persons employed at the time of the 2009 ASEC Supplement received unemployment compensation in 2008. But 6.3% of the employed lived in a household with income in 2008 that was below the official poverty level.

a. A person is unemployed if they are not working, have actively looked for work during the four weeks before the CPS is conducted, and are currently available for work. The long-term unemployed are persons who have been unemployed for 27 weeks or more.

b. Public assistance consists of cash payments under the Temporary Assistance for Needy Families (TANF) program, state and local general assistance programs, and other forms of cash assistance.

Poverty

Poverty is a common measure of economic well-being. In 2008, almost a third (31.0%) of the long-term unemployed lived in households that had incomes below the official poverty level. This percentage was not statistically different from either 2001 (27.1%) or 1991 (27.4%). (See **Table 1**.)

Public Assistance and Supplemental Nutrition Assistance

Households that receive public assistance or benefits under the Supplemental Nutrition Assistance Program (SNAP, formerly the Food Stamp program) have low incomes. In 2008, about one in five (20.3%) long-term unemployed workers lived in a household where someone received SNAP benefits. This was higher than in 2001 (15.7%) but statistically the same as in 1991 (19.3%).

In 2008, only 2.7% of the long-term unemployed received income from public assistance.[29] This percentage was down from an estimated 4.3% in 2001 and 7.6% in 1991. Public assistancecaseloads for 1991 and 2001 are not comparable, however. The number of families receiving cash welfare assistance declined after Congress enacted the Temporary Aid to Needy Families (TANF) program in 1996.[30] In addition, the CPS may underestimate the percentage of unemployed who receive public assistance. A comparison of estimates from the CPS with administrative data from the TANF program suggests that the CPS does not capture a significant portion of persons who receive public assistance and that this underreporting has worsened over time.[31] (See Table 1.)

HealthInsuranceCoverage

Unemployed workers may lose employer contributions for health insurance. [32] They may, however, be eligible for coverage under Medicaid, be covered by the insurance policy of a family member, or buy insurance through their former employer or directly from an insurer.

The American Recovery and Reinvestment Act of 2009 (ARRA, P.L. 111-5) included a subsidy for up to 15 months for unemployed workers who buy health insurance under COBRA. The subsidy is available to workers who lost their jobs between September 1, 2008, and March 31, 2010. The subsidy consists of an employer tax credit equal to 65% of the unemployed worker's health insurance premium. [33]

Some unemployed workers may be eligible for a health coverage income tax credit (HCTC), which may bolster the share with benefits. The credit against health insurance premiums is available to workers who are receiving income or wage subsidies under the TAA program or are between the ages of 55 and 64 and are receiving payments from the Pension Benefit Guaranty Corporation (PBGC).[34]

In 2008, as shown in Table 1, approximately 15.5% of long-term unemployed workers were covered by Medicaid. Statistically, this percentage was not different from either 2001 (12.8%) or 1991 (11.1%).

Figure 12 shows that an estimated 55% of long-term unemployed had health insurance coverage at some time during 2008. This is significantly less than the 84% of employed workers who had insurance coverage. It is also less than the percentage of long-term unemployed who had health insurance coverage in 2001 (60.3%) but statistically the same as in 1991 (57.3%).

Number of Earners in the Household

Many households have more than one member who is employed. If a worker becomes unemployed, other household members may continue to work, work more hours, or enter the workforce. In 2008, however, one-fourth of the households of the long-term unemployed had no earned income. As shown in Table 2, the percentage with no earners in 2008 was higher than in 2001 (17.2%) but not statistically different from 1991 (22.5%).

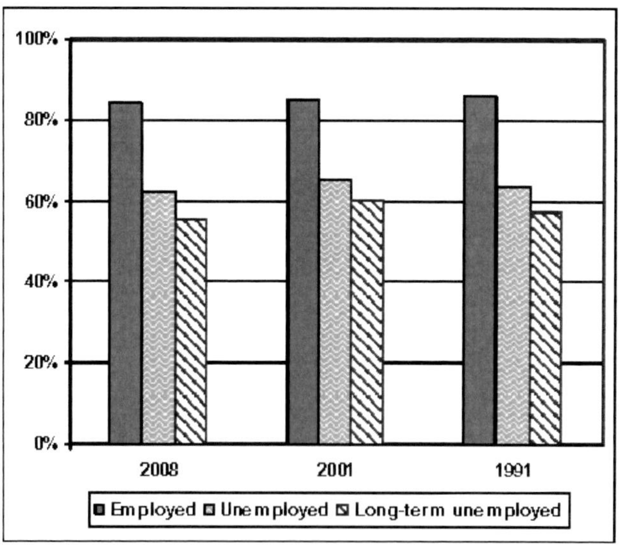

Source: CRS analysis of data from the Annual Social and Economic (ASEC) Supplement to the Current Population Survey (CPS).

Figure 12. Percentage of Individuals with Health Insurance Coverage, 2008, 2001, and 1991.

Table 2. Number of Earners in the Households of the Employed, Unemployed, andLong-Term Unemployed, 2008, 2001, and 1991(Percent)

Labor Force Status of Individual	Number of Earners	2008	2001	1991
All Households				
Employed	No earners[a]	1.0	1.0	0.9
	One earner	47.6	45.9	44.1
	Two earners	41.5	42.3	42.7
	Three or more earners	9.9	10.9	12.3
Unemployed	No earners	9.9	8.2	10.8
	One earner	51.8	51.6	47.5
	Two earners	30.8	32.8	34.5
	Three or more earners	7.4	7.4	7.2
Long-Term Unemployed	No earners	24.9	17.2	22.5
	One earner	48.4	51.9	41.2
	Two earners	21.6	25.9	29.8
	Three or more earners	5.1	4.9	6.5
Married Couples Only				
Employed	No earners	0.4	0.3	0.5
	One earner	18.0	17.6	20.1
	Two earners	65.7	64.8	60.6
	Three or more earners	15.9	17.3	18.9
Unemployed	No earners	2.1	2.2	4.1
	One earner	26.9	23.5	27.6
	Two earners	57.2	61.0	55.1
	Three or more earners	13.8	13.3	13.2
Long-Term Unemployed	No earners	4.2	7.4	12.2
	One earner	40.3	33.6	31.5
	Two earners[a]	43.3	49.9	44.4
	Three or more earners	12.3	9.1	12.0

Source: CRS analysis of data from the Annual Social and Economic (ASEC) Supplement to the Current Population Survey (CPS).

Note: Percentages may not add to 100% because of rounding.

a. The ASEC Supplement collects earnings information for both wage and salary workers and self-employed persons. Some self-employed workers report negative earnings if the losses from their business are greater than their wages. In this chapter, workers with negative earnings are not counted as earners. Only workers with positive earnings are counted as earners.

If a single parent or single individual becomes unemployed, there may not be anyone else in the household with earnings. Among married couples, if one spouse becomes unemployed, the other spouse (or someone else in the household) may be working or may go to work.

Among married couples in 2008, only 4.2% of the families of the long-term unemployed had no earned income in 2008. This percentage was not statistically different from 2001 (7.4%), but was lower than in 1991 (12.2%). The decline since 1991 may be due to a number of factors, including the lack of data for 2009, an increase in the labor force participation rate of married women, a change in the average age of married persons, and changes in the size and composition of married couple households.[35]

Homeownership

Employed workers are more likely than unemployed workers to own their own home. Nevertheless, a majority of unemployed workers regardless of unemployment duration arehomeowners. Figure 13 shows that, in 2008, 72% of employed workers owned their own home, compared to 57% of unemployed workers and 58% of the long-term unemployed.[36]

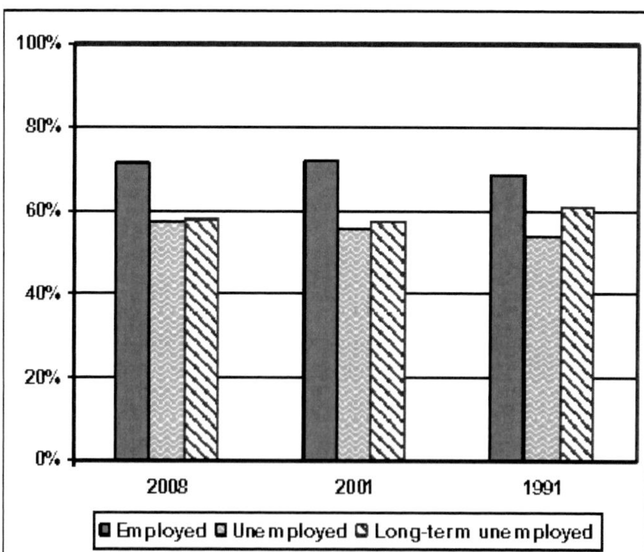

Source: CRS analysis of data from the Annual Social and Economic (ASEC) Supplement to the Current Population Survey (CPS).

Figure 13. Percentage of Individuals Who are Homeowners, 2008, 2001, and 1991.

From 1991 to 2008, homeownership fell among workers who were unemployed for more than six months (from 61% to 58%). However, homeownership rose among employed workers (from 69% to 72%) and for all unemployed workers (from 54% to 57%). From 2001 to 2008, there were no significant changes in the percentages of employed, unemployed, or long-term unemployed workers who owned their own homes.

Job loss and a reduction in household income may cause some borrowers to become delinquent on their mortgage loans. A borrower who has missed three or more mortgage payments is generally considered to be in default. After a default, lenders may take a number of steps— including rescheduling loan payments or restructuring a loan—before proceeding to foreclosure (i.e., a lender may recover losses on a loan by repossessing the home).[37] At the end of 2009, the percentage of mortgages that were 90 or more days past due accounted for over half of all delinquent loans, double the percentage from a year earlier.[38] For this chapter, the most recent data on homeownership are for 2008. Data for 2009 may or may not show a change in homeownership from 2008 for either unemployed workers or the long-term unemployed

IMPLICATIONS FOR PUBLIC POLICY

Recessions are generally characterized by a drop in consumer demand and a decline in investment. Consumers buy fewer cars and homes, and cut back on purchases from retail stores, for example. For their part, businesses invest less in new buildings and equipment. A result of the decline in aggregate demand is an increase in unemployment. Fiscal and monetary policy are the macroeconomic responses to a recession. Fiscal policy consists of changes in government spending and taxes. Monetary policy consists of actions by the Federal Reserve to affect the supply of money and interest rates.[39]

The strength of an economic rebound largely determines the pace of net job growth (i.e., the extent to which additions exceed separations from employer payrolls) and reduction in unemployment, including long-term unemployment. In the early stages of an economic recovery, increased demand for goods and services first slows the flow of workers into unemployment. While short-term unemployment consequently falls, the average duration of unemployment increases for some time following a recession's end. Once employers become confident that an economic upturn is firmly in place, they go beyond restoring the hours worked by employees whom they retained during the recession to hire additional workers.

But, a return to economic growth may not be sufficient to fully overcome the reemployment problems of the long-term unemployed. Employers may rank job applicants by their duration of unemployment and hire from the front of the queue (i.e., the short-term unemployed) because they consider lengthy unemployment to be a signal of poor worker quality (i.e., low productivity). In effect, long-term unemployment stigmatizes workers. Firms may also be reluctant to hire the long-term unemployed because they believe the group's skills have atrophied during their lengthy time away from the workplace. In addition, businesses may discriminate against older workers who, as previously described, are more likely than younger workers to be among the long-term unemployed.

A variety of employment policies might be considered to ameliorate these labor market difficulties. Offering wage subsidies to firms that hire the long-term unemployed compensates employers for the group's actual or perceived skill shortcomings.[40] So, too, does providing a training subsidy to companies that hire workers with arguably deteriorated skills due to their lengthy bout of unemployment.[41] Passage of a temporary public jobs program early in a recession may prevent the skill erosion potentially induced by long-term unemployment. The latter was one of the rationales for enacting job creation programs during the Great Depression.[42] And,employers might be discouraged from failing to hire older displaced workers through stepped up enforcement of workplace discrimination laws.[43]

A return to economic growth also may be insufficient to fully overcome the reemployment problems of the long-term unemployed given the history of structural change coinciding with cyclical downturns. Before the back-to-back recessions of the early 1 980s, for example, workers in the steel industry were about half as likely as the average worker to experience long-term unemployment. With the advent of these recessions, long-term unemployment among steelworkers became "among the worst of any worker group. ...Considerable evidence indicates that the Nation's steel industry is suffering from some basic problems quite unrelated to cyclical declines in demand."[44]

One approach that has been suggested to reemploy workers displaced from jobs in restructuring industries is wage insurance. Such a program may encourage high-tenure, high-wage workers to accept lower paying jobs in growing industries by compensating them for the difference in wages from their new and old jobs. Under the Alternative Trade Adjustment Assistance (ATAA) program, older workers who become reemployed within 26 weeks of being laid off can receive one-half of the difference in earnings from their former and new jobs up to a maximum of $10,000 over two years.[45]

Another potential policy response is providing reemployment bonuses to unemployed workers who accept new jobs within a given time frame, thereby shortening their spell of unemployment. Experiments were conducted in a few states in the 1980s to evaluate the efficacy of variously designed reemployment bonus programs. The evaluations and subsequent reanalyses generally concluded that offering bonuses to UC recipients shortened their length of benefit receipt, especially when UC recipients also were offered job search assistance and when the bonus programs were targeted at those UC recipients most likely to exhaust their benefits.[46]

If restructuring industries are concentrated geographically, then economic development and relocation assistance may be appropriate measures as well. But, these strategies do not necessarily focus on assisting the long-term unemployed. States typically take the lead in efforts to attract growing industries to reemploy their laid off residents. To assist the workers and communities adversely affected by the auto industry's restructuring, however, President Obama created the position of Director of Recovery for Auto Communities and Workers within the Department of Labor to leverage available federal resources (e.g., ARRA funds). In contrast, providing assistance to unemployed workers to encourage them to take jobs in other areas is not often mentioned today. Relocation assistance currently is one of the benefits offered to TAA-eligible workers, those receiving Department of Labor national emergency grants, and adult and dislocated workers served by the Workforce Investment Act.

Lastly, workers laid off due to structural changes in the economy may not possess the skills needed to get jobs in expanding industries. While these individuals can undertake education and training to acquire the requisite skills, these activities may not result in reemploying the long-term unemployed as quickly as some of the approaches discussed above.

Appendix. Data and Methodology

The analysis in this chapter is based on data from the Current Population Survey (CPS), which is a household survey conducted by the U.S. Census Bureau for the Bureau of Labor Statistics (BLS). The monthly CPS is the source of the national unemployment rate and other labor market information.

The survey is representative of the civilian, noninstitutional population. The sample does not include persons living in institutions (such as mental hospitals, nursing homes, or correctional facilities). The monthly survey does not include individuals who are on active duty in the military. The monthly sample includes approximately 60,000 households.[47]

Each year, the CPS conducts the Annual Social and Economic (ASEC) supplement to the monthly CPS. The supplement collects information on the types and sources of family income, health insurance coverage, and other household information. The supplement collects information for the previous year. The sample for the ASEC supplement is representative of the civilian, noninstitutional population of the United States. The sample for the supplement includesmembers of the Armed Forces living in civilian housing units on a military base or in a household not on a military base. The 2009 supplement collected information from about 76,200 households.[48]

In the supplement, earnings include wage and salary income and income from self-employment. Wages and salaries include earnings from self-employment, tips, commissions, and cash bonuses. Total income includes earnings, interest and dividends, social security and pension benefits, public assistance, unemployment and worker's compensation, alimony and child support, and other types of money income. Money income does not include in-kind transfers for food, housing, healthcare, or energy assistance. Money income does not include capital gains and is income before taxes or other deductions. [49] In this chapter, total family earnings and income consist of the sum of earnings and income of all persons in a household or married couple family.

In the CPS, a family is defined as a group of two or more persons who are living together and who are related by birth, marriage, or adoption.[50] In the CPS, a family may include a related subfamily, such as a married son or daughter or an unmarried son or daughter with a child. The CPS defines single individuals as either "nonfamily householders" or "secondary individuals." Following the CPS definition of a family, in this chapter married couples and single parent families may include one or more related subfamilies. A primary family and an unrelated subfamily living in the same household are treated as two separate families. Unmarried parents are treated as a single parent and a single individual. Unmarried couples without children are treated as two single individuals.

The analysis in this chapter includes persons in the labor force, either employed or unemployed, who are ages 16 or over. The analysis of household and family earnings and income includes households and families with positive earnings or income.

Topcoding

To protect the confidentiality of survey participants, the CPS assigns an income amount to higher income persons. Changes in these amounts, or topcodes, over time can affect the observed trend in real income and earnings. For example, in 1991, individual earnings were topcoded at $99,999; in 2001, earnings were topcoded at $150,000; and in 2008, earnings were topcoded at $200,000. Since 1996, for persons with earnings above the topcoded amounts, the amount of earnings reported in the public CPS files is the average earnings of workers with similar characteristics. Average earnings are calculated for persons based on gender, race, ethnicity, and whether or not a person works full-time, year-round. Since 1999, for persons with incomes above the topcoded amounts, the public CPS files report the average income of persons with topcoded income. For consistency, for the years 2001 and 2008, this chapter uses average topcoded earnings and income as reported in the CPS and, for 1991, average earnings and income from a report published by the National Bureau of Economic Research (NBER).[51]

Confidence Intervals

Estimates based on survey responses from a sample of households have two kinds of error: nonsampling and sampling. Examples of nonsampling error include information that is misreported and errors made in processing collected information. Sampling error occurs because a sample, and not the entire population, of households is surveyed. The difference between an estimate based on a sample of households and the actual population value is known as sampling error. When using sample data, researchers typically construct confidence intervals around population estimates. Confidence intervals provide information about the accuracy of estimated values. With a 90% confidence interval and repeated samples from a population, 90% of intervals will include the average estimate of the population characteristic.

End Notes

[1] Michael A. Fletcher and Dana Hedgpeth, "Are Unemployment Benefits No Longer Temporary?," *Washington Post*, March 9, 2010, pp. A1, A11.

[2] For additional information, see CRS Report RS22915, *Temporary Extension of Unemployment Benefits: Emergency Unemployment Compensation (EUC08)*, by Katelin P. Isaacs, Julie M. Whittaker, and Alison M. Shelton.

[3] CRS Report R40798, *Unemployment and Employment Trends Before and After the End of Recessions*, by Linda Levine.

[4] Calculated by the Congressional Research Service (CRS) from the Current Population Survey (CPS). Individuals are counted as unemployed if they are not working, have actively looked for work during the four weeks before the CPS survey, and are currently available for work.

[5] The National Bureau of Economic Research is the official arbiter of turning points in the business cycle. It typically has not announced the starting and ending dates of recessions until well after the fact. For purposes of comparison with prior recessions, August 2009 was used in this chapter as the month in which the latest recession may have ended because it is the consensus among economists that the business cycle reached its nadir in the third quarter of 2009.

[6] Data derived by BLS from the CPS.

[7] The long-term unemployment rate exceeded 2.6% starting in May 2009; 2.6% was the previous record-high for the postwar period. It was reached in June 1983, seven months after the end of the 1981-1982 recession.

[8] The Extended Benefit (EB) program is automatically triggered when a state surpasses a statutorily set unemployment rate. Workers in high-unemployment states are eligible for up to 20 weeks of benefits beyond the duration provided under their state's UC program (typically 26 weeks). With ARRA, as amended, temporarily paying 100% of EB costs, many workers unemployed during this recession were eligible for the EB benefit as well as the EUC benefit. Additionally, during prior recessions when Congress enacted a temporary unemployment benefit program, states were allowed to suspend the EB program.

[9] The peak rate rather than the rate at the end of recessions was used in the analysis because in five instances, the temporary federal UC program was enacted after the trough and in two instances, it was enacted very near the trough. Only in the latest case did Congress enact the program well before the recession's end. According to CRS Report RL34340, *Extending Unemployment Compensation Benefits During Recessions*, Congress provided a maximum of 13 weeks of benefits in response to four recessions: 1957-1958, 1960-1961, 1969-1970, and 2001. The peak long-term unemployment rates and peak shares of long-term unemployment after the end of these recessions ranged from 0.8% to 1.5% and from 13.6% to 23.4%, respectively. Congress provided 26 weeks of benefits in response to the severe 1973- 1975 recession; the long-term unemployment peaked at 1.7% and the share of long-term unemployment peaked at 21.1% after the recession's end. Congress next provided 16 weeks of benefits in response to the severe 1981-1982 recession; both the long-term unemployment rate (2.6%) and the share of long-term unemployment (25.7%) exceeded the rates attained after Congress provided UC benefits for shorter (13 weeks) and longer (26 weeks) periods. Until the 2007-2009 recession, the longest period for which temporary federal UC benefits were authorized came in response to the 1990-1991 recession. Despite the 33-week benefit period, the peak long-term unemployment rate (1.7%) and peak share of long-term unemployment (23.3%) after the end of the 1990-1991 recession were comparable to figures associated with shorter UC extensions.

[10] The official count of unemployment is developed by the BLS from the CPS, not from UC administrative records that cover a subset of unemployed persons who are benefit-eligible. (In 2009, according to Labor Department data, insured unemployment accounted for 40% of total unemployment.) Nonetheless, it is likely that survey respondents are saying that more

unemployed members of their households are seeking work than would have been case in the absence of EUC program.

[11] Rob Valletta and Katherine Kuang, "Extended Unemployment and UI Benefits," *FRBSF Economic Letter*, no. 20 10-12 (April 19, 2010).

[12] BLS, "Job Openings and Labor Turnover—February 2010," *News Release*, April 6, 2010.

[13] When unemployment occurs because of a mismatch between the skills supplied by workers and the skills demanded by employers, it is called structural unemployment. In contrast, cyclical unemployment results from the temporarily reduced demand for labor that occurs during recessions when the demand for goods and services is depressed.

[14] Erica Groshen and Simon Potter, "Has Structural Change Contributed to a Jobless Recovery," *Federal Reserve Bank of New York Current Issues in Economics and Finance*, vol. 9, no. 8 (August 2003), pp. 1-7.

[15] Daniel Aaronson, Ellen R. Rissman, and Daniel G. Sullivan, "Can Sectoral Reallocation Explain the Jobless Recovery," *Federal Reserve Bank of Chicago Economic Perspectives*, vol. 28, no. 2 (second quarter 2004), pp. 36-49.

[16] Andrew Figura and William Wascher, "The Causes and Consequences of Sectoral Reallocation: Evidence from the Early 21st Century," *Business Economics*, vol. 45, no. 1 (2010), pp.49-68.

[17] Ellen R. Rissman, "Employment Growth: Cyclical Movements or Structural Change?," *Federal Reserve Bank of Chicago Economic Perspectives*, fourth quarter 2009, pp. 40-57.

[18] In a 2007 report, the Congressional Budget Office (CBO) examined the extent to which unemployment is concentrated among workers who are unemployed for more than six months. The report examined the characteristics of workers who experienced unemployment at any time from 2001 to 2003. Although the report uses data from the monthly CPS, it mainly uses data from the 2001 panel of the Survey of Income and Program Participation (SIPP). SIPP is a longitudinal survey of the population of the United States and is conducted by the U.S. Census Bureau. Unlike the CBO study, this chapter examines the characteristics of the long-term unemployed during recent recessions. (Congressional Budget Office, *Long-Term Unemployment*, October 2007, pp. vii, 21.)

[19] For information on the reemployment problems faced by older workers who lose long-held jobs, see CRS Report RL33054, *Older Displaced Workers in the Context of an Aging and Slowly Growing Population*, by Linda Levine.

[20]AysegulSahin, Joseph Song, and Bart Hobijn, "The Unemployment Gender Gap during the 2007 Recession," *Federal Reserve Bank of New York Current Issues in Economics and Finance*, vol. 16, no. 2 (February 2010). (Hereafter cited as "The Unemployment Gender Gap.")

[21] Unless otherwise noted, the percentage comparisons in this chapter are significant at the 90% confidence level or better. See the discussion of confidence intervals in the Appendix.

[22] Another contributory factor may be the 1994 revision of the CPS, which led to more women reporting they were unemployed rather than not being members of the labor force.

[23] Unpublished BLS data from the Current Population Survey (CPS).

[24] Calculated by CRS from BLS establishment survey data.

[25] In 2009, office and administrative support workers accounted for 13.0% of total employment. They accounted for a larger share of employment in the information industry (18.6%) and in the financial activities industry (24.6%), according to CRS calculations utilizing BLS data from the CPS.

[26] U.S. Census Bureau, *Current Population Survey, 2009 Annual Social and Economic (ASEC) Supplement*, available at http://www.census.gov/apsd/techdoc/cps/cpsmar09.pdf, p. 9-4. (Hereafter cited as U.S. Census Bureau, *Current Population Survey, 2009 Annual Social and Economic (ASEC) Supplement.*)

[27] The 2009 ASEC Supplement asks survey participants the following question: "At any time during 2008 did (name/you) receive any State or Federal unemployment compensation?"

U.S. Census Bureau, *Current Population Survey, 2009 Annual Social and Economic (ASEC) Supplement*, p. D-20.

[28] Estimates for 2008 may not be comparable to estimates for 2001 or 1991, the official end dates of the two previous recessions. NBER has not announced the official end date of the recent recession, but many economists believe that it will be in the third quarter of 2009.

[29] Public assistance consists of cash payments under the Temporary Assistance for Needy Families (TANF) program, state and local general assistance programs, and other forms of cash assistance.

[30] See CRS Report RL32760, *The Temporary Assistance for Needy Families (TANF) Block Grant: Responses to Frequently Asked Questions*, by Gene Falk.

[31] See CRS Report RL3 0797, *Trends in Welfare, Work, and the Economic Well-Being of Female-Headed Families with Children: 1987-2008*, by Thomas Gabe.

[32] For information on employer-provided fringe benefits, see CRS Report RL33 835, *Real Earnings, Health Insurance and Pension Coverage, and the Distribution of Earnings, 1979-2007*, by Gerald Mayer.

[33] Both the House and Senate have passed legislation that would extend the eligibility period for the COBRA subsidy. On December 16, 2009, the House passed H.R. 2847, the Jobs for Mainstreet Act, 2010, which would extend the COBRA subsidy to workers who lose their jobs through June 30, 2010. On March 10, 2010, the Senate passed H.R. 4213, the American Workers, State and Business Relief Act, which would extend eligibility for COBRA subsidies to workers who lose their jobs through December 31, 2010. See CRS Report R40165, *Unemployment and Health Insurance: Current Legislation and Issues*, by JanemarieMulvey.

[34] For more information on the HCTC, see CRS Report RL32620, *Health Coverage Tax Credit*, by Bernadette Fernandez. Beginning in 2014, the Patient Protection and Affordable Care Act (H.R. 3590, P.L. 111-148) would provide subsidies to individuals and families with incomes between 133% and 400% of the federal poverty level who buy health insurance through new insurance exchanges. CRS Report R40942, *Private Health Insurance Provisions in the Patient Protection and Affordable Care Act (PPACA)*, by HindaChaikind et al..

[35] From 1991 to 2008, the labor force participation rate of women increased from 57.4% to 59.5%. For men, it declined from 75.8% to 73.0%. Bureau of Labor Statistics, *Labor Force Statistics from the Current Population Survey*, available at http://stats.bls.gov/cps/.

[36] Most households that do not own their homes are renters. A small percentage of households neither own nor rent. They receive nonmoney income from their employer in the form of rent free housing.

[37] See CRS Report RL34232, *The Process, Data, and Costs of Mortgage Foreclosure*, coordinated by Darryl E. Getter, and CRS Report R40210, *Preserving Homeownership: Foreclosure Prevention Initiatives*, by Katie Jones.

[38] Renae Merle, "Mortgage Delinquency Rate Slows in Fourth Quarter," *Washington Post*, February 20, 2010.

[39] Fiscal policy (i.e., budget surpluses or deficits) may also affect interest rates.

[40] For example, P.L. 111-147 includes a provision temporarily reducing the payroll tax of employers who hire persons unemployed for 60 days or more. (For additional information, see CRS Report R41006, *Unemployment: Issues and Policies*, by Jane G. Gravelle, Thomas L. Hungerford, and Marc Labonte.) Other legislation was introduced to add the long-term unemployed to the groups for whom an employer can claim the Work Opportunity Tax Credit. (For additional information, see CRS Report RL3 0089, *The Work Opportunity Tax Credit (WOTC)*, by Linda Levine.)

[41] For information about on-the-job training under the Workforce Investment Act, see CRS Report R41 135, *The Workforce Investment Act and the One-Stop Delivery System*, by David H. Bradley.

[42] For additional information on two of these programs, see CRS Report R41017, *Job Creation Programs of the Great Depression: the WPA and the CCC*, by Linda Levine.

[43] For additional information, see CRS Report RL34652, *The Age Discrimination in Employment Act (ADEA): A Legal Overview*, by Jody Feder.

[44] Philip L. Rones, "Recent Recessions Swell Ranks of the Long-Term Unemployed," *Monthly Labor Review*, February 1984, pp. 25-29.

[45] For additional information on the ATAA program, see CRS Report RL34383, *Trade Adjustment Assistance (TAA) for Workers: Current Issues and Legislation*, by John J. Topoleski.

[46] For additional information, see CRS Report RL3 1825, *Personal Reemployment Accounts: Results from Bonus Experiments*, by Linda Levine and Ann Lordeman.

[47] Bureau of Labor Statistics, "Labor Force Data Derived from the Current Population Survey," *Handbook of Methods*, available at http://www.bls.gov/opub/hom/pdf/homch1.pdf, pp. 1-2.

[48] U.S. Census Bureau, *Current Population Survey, 2009 Annual Social and Economic (ASEC) Supplement*, pp. 1-1, 9- 3, G-3.

[49] Ibid., p. 9-4.

[50] Ibid., p. 9-2.

[51] Jeff Larrimore, Richard V. Burkhauser, ShuaizhangFeng, and Laura Zayatz, *Consistent Cell Means for Topcoded Incomes in the Public Use March CPS (1976-2007)*, NBER, Working Paper 13941, April 2008, available at http://www.nber.org/papers/w13941, p. 46. U.S. Census Bureau, *Current Population Survey, 2009 Annual Social and Economic (ASEC) Supplement*, p. 5-1.

In: Recession, Depression, and Unemployment ISBN: 978-1-61761-508-5
Editors: Daniel A. García

Chapter 2

JOB LOSS AND INFRASTRUCTURE JOB CREATION SPENDING DURING THE RECESSION

Linda Levine

SUMMARY

After the long economic expansion that characterized much of the current decade, the nation entered its 11th postwar recession in December 2007. The subsequent decrease in jobs and comparison of the latest recession to the Great Depression intensified congressional interest in passing legislation early in 2009 aimed at encouraging creation of new jobs and warding off further loss of jobs.

To mitigate all but one recession since the 1960s, Congress chose to increase federal spending on public works (infrastructure). (See CRS Report 92-93 9, *Countercyclical Job Creation Programs*.) Public works expenditures traditionally have gone to certain types of construction activities (e.g., building highways and bridges, dams and flood control structures) which indirectly increase demand in industries that supply their products to construction firms (e.g., manufacturing). Today, the definition of infrastructure has been expanded to include green economic activities (commonly referred to as green jobs), which include industries that utilize renewable resources (e.g., electricity generated by wind), produce energy-efficient goods and services(e.g., mass transit), and install energy-conserving products (e.g., retrofitting buildings with thermal-pane windows).

A question that typically arises during congressional consideration of economic stimulus legislation is which approach produces the most bang for the buck. In the instant case, this means how many jobs might be supported by federal expenditures on traditional and green infrastructure projects. Once stimulus legislation is signed into law, the focus of Congress customarily turns to estimates of the number of jobs that result as federal funds are allocated to specific activities. Therefore, after briefly examining the trend in employment since the recession's onset, the report turns to an in-depth look at estimates of job creation, including the limitations of the methodology often used to derive them and the difficulties associated with developing job estimates for green infrastructure in particular.

The report closes with a review of what is known to date about the number of jobs supported by infrastructure spending and other provisions in the American Recovery and Reinvestment Act (ARRA, P.L. 111-5). Section 1512 requires entities that receive ARRA appropriations from federal agencies, totaling approximately $271 billion, to include in quarterly reports to the agencies the number of direct jobs created or maintained as a result. Recipients of ARRA funds awarded by the Department of Transportation (DOT) must comply with the Section 1512 job reporting requirement; in addition, Section 1201 of P.L. 111-5 requires the DOT to estimate the direct, indirect, and total jobs associated with ARRA-funded transportation projects. Section 1513 of the act requires the Council of Economic Advisers (CEA) to report quarterly on the effect of ARRA provisions on employment and other economic indicators. The CEA's reports are the most comprehensive because they contain estimates of not only jobs supported by ARRA appropriations but also of jobs associated with other parts of P.L. 111-5 (e.g., unemployment and health insurance benefits, state fiscal relief, and tax provisions).

After the long economic expansion that characterized much of the current decade, the nation entered its 11th postwar recession in December 2007. It was not until November 2008, however, that the Business Cycle Dating Committee of the National Bureau of Economic Research announced that a substantial and widespread decline in economic activity had begun a year earlier. As part of its announcement, the committee noted that it "views the payroll employment measure, which is based on a large survey of employers, as the most reliable comprehensive estimate of employment. This series [the CES] reached a peak in December 2007."

The committee's announcement intensified congressional interest in passage of legislation aimed at encouraging creation of new jobs and warding off further loss of jobs. So, too, did comments equating the recession to the Great Depression. (See CRS Report R40655, *The Labor Market During the Great Depression and the Current Recession.*) This, in turn, sparked the interest of some policymakers in the job creation programs of the Depression period. (See CRS Report R4 1017, *Job Creation Programs of the Great Depression: the WPA and the CCC.*)

To mitigate all but one recession since the 1960s, Congress chose to increase federal expenditures on infrastructure (public works), thereby directly raising demand for goods and services to offset the reduced demand of consumers. (See CRS Report 92-939, *Countercyclical Job Creation Programs.*) But, there are a number of issues associated with using spending on public works to quickly create jobs during a recession. (See CRS Report R40107, *The Role of Public Works Infrastructure in Economic Stimulus.*)

When Congress considers spending on infrastructure to help stimulate a flagging economy, "how many jobs are created" is a commonly asked question. After first briefly examining trends in employment since the latest recession began, this chapter focuses on job creation estimates available in late 2008 associated with increased spending on traditional and so-called green infrastructure, placing a heavy emphasis on explaining the methodology often used to derive them and the difficulties associated with developing estimates for green economic activities in particular.

Once stimulus legislation is signed into law, the focus of Congress customarily turns to estimates of the number of jobs that result as federal funds are allocated to specific activities. In the case of the American Recovery and Reinvestment Act (ARRA, P.L. 111-5), which was enacted in early 2009, Congress included language requiring entities that receive ARRA appropriations from federal agencies to report the number of jobs created or maintained as a result and requiring the Council of Economic Advisers to report on the employment and other economic effects of ARRA provisions. The report closes with a review of what is known to date about the number of jobs associated with the stimulus act.

Net Job Loss

Total nonfarm employment declined steadily between December 2007 and October 2009, falling from 137,951,000 to 129,633,000. The great majority of this 8,318,000 job loss occurred after November 2008. Despite a small uptick in employment from October to November 2009, the number of jobs on employer payrolls fell the following month. Firms have been increasing their employment since then, however, with the number of jobs in April 2010 preliminarily rising to 130,161,000.

As is typical during economic downturns, employees in the goods-producing sector (mining, construction, manufacturing) have been the most adversely affected. Workers in the sector's construction industry began experiencing job losses even before the economy-wide downturn began.

Employment in the service-providing sector most recently peaked in December 2007, when the recession began. Some service-providing industries—utilities, education and health services— have continued to add workers. But, job losses elsewhere in the sector have far outweighed their gains. The financial activities industry began to lose jobs before the advent of the economy-wide downturn. This mirrors the above-mentioned trend in construction employment in part because real estate is a component of financial activities and it, like construction, has been hurt by the collapse of the housing market. Other components of financial activities, such as brokerage firms that packaged high-risk mortgages and the investors (e.g., banks) that purchased them, have been negatively affected by the housing market downturn as well.

Despite the widely expressed belief that the recession ended sometime in the third quarter of 2009, the pattern following the end of the prior 10 postwar recessions suggests that an uninterrupted rebound in jobs will not be immediate. According to a CRS analysis, in all but one of these recessions,

> the number of jobs on employer payrolls fluctuated for months.... Sustained job growth occurred within three to five months of the start of seven recoveries. In sharp contrast, steady job growth did not commence until March 1992—12 months after the July 1990–March 1991 recession ended— and not until September 2003—22 months after the March– November 2001 recession ended.[1]

INFRASTRUCTURE SPENDING AND JOB CREATIONESTIMATES

When in response to a recession Congress has acted to create jobs by raising demand for goods and services through increased federal spending, it often has chosen to direct the funds to infrastructure (public works) activities. Other means of direct countercyclical job creation— public service employment, fiscal relief to state governments, and employment tax credits—have been relied on much less often.[2]

Historically, public works has been synonymous with heavy and civil construction activities (e.g., road and bridge building, flood control structures and dam building). Today, it includes green economic activities or so-called green jobs. Although numerous studies on the emerging green economy have been released in the last several years, no consistent definition of green jobs exists at present. Green jobs seemingly are those in and related to industries that utilize renewable resources to produce their outputs (e.g., energy generated by wind, solar, and geothermal technologies) and jobs in and related to industries that produce energy-efficient goods (e.g., Energy Star appliances) and services (e.g., mass transit).[3] For this reason, the following discussion focuses on what is known about the job-generating impact of infrastructure spending broadly defined.

The section below begins with an in-depth examination of how job creation estimates usually are developed. The focus then narrows to look at two models that can be used to calculate the number of jobs nationwide dependent upon demand in the construction industry among others, and one model that can be used to calculate the number of jobs by state dependent on the construction industry among other industries. The section ends by reviewing the difficulties that researchers encounter in estimating the number of jobs supported by expenditures on green economic activities and the consequent caution that should be taken when utilizing these estimates in particular.

Job Creation Estimates: What Are They?

Interest in how many jobs are created by a particular type of economic activity has surfaced when the economy is in a downturn and policymakers seek to compare the relative advantages of different stimulus options. It also has arisen when policymakers want to know the impact of shifting expenditures from one federal budget category to another (e.g., away from defense and towards social services programs). Unless there is an *increase* in total spending, however, the number of jobs in the labor market would remain largely unchanged.[4]

Although there are other bases upon which to develop estimates of the number of jobs created by a given economic activity, an input-output (I-O) model of the economy often is utilized due to its cost-effectiveness.[5] An I-O model describes the interrelationships between industries in the production process, showing how the dollar value of a sale is distributed across industries at a particular point in time. It thus reflects how much of the purchased product comes from final and supplier industries. An I-O table might show, for example, the dollar value of roof trusses produced by the veneer, plywood, and engineered wood products manufacturing industry and the dollar value of bricks produced by the clay product and refractory manufacturing industry used by the construction industry to erect residential buildings.

The output requirements from each industry must then be converted to employment requirements. Employment requirements are derived from productivity estimates for each industry at a particular point in time. The total employment requirement associated with a given type of final demand (e.g., a water reuse program) is the employment in the industry producing the final product or service and in the supplier industries. In other words, it is an approximation of both the direct and indirect employment dependent upon/supported by the economic activity. It commonly is expressed as the number of jobs per billion dollars of expenditures valued in a particular year's dollars.

Like an I-O table, an employment requirements table is a matrix of hundreds of columns and rows. Each column displays the number of jobs supported in each of the industry rows by an expenditure of one billion dollars in the column industry. For example, one billion dollars spent in the construction industry supports (direct) employment in the various components of that industry (e.g., residential and commercial building, highway and bridge building) and (indirect) employment in the many industries that supply their goods and services to the construction industry (e.g., asphalt shingle manufacturing, fabricated metal bridge section manufacturing). An employment requirements table thus permits estimation of the varying impact of an expenditure on different industries and the varying impact of different kinds of expenditures.

SomeCaveats

I-O models freeze technology and productivity at a particular point in time. Thus, the job- generating potential of an economic activity undertaken today could differ from that of an earlier period if there were technological and productivity improvements in the intervening years. Similarly, the estimates often are stated in terms of the number of jobs created for every billion dollars of expenditures, but a billion dollars spent in one year could buy less (or more) than a billion dollars spent in another year depending on changes in price levels over time.

There also could be differences in estimated versus actual job creation because I-O models assume that resources are unlimited. If, for example, the economy was performing at a fairly high level with plants operating near full capacity and with fairly few workers unemployed, the actual number of new jobs might fall short of the estimate due to capital and labor constraints. This is less likely to matter during a broad-based economic downturn.

Further, I-O tables do not necessarily differentiate between imported and domestically produced goods. As a consequence, the domestic employment impact of expenditures might be overstated to the extent that inputs are imported. Similarly, I-O tables typically do not express employment in terms of full-time equivalents (i.e., both full-time and part-time jobs are counted equally). Thus, programs which draw upon industries that rely relatively more on part-time workers (e.g., retail trade) might appear to create more jobs than programs that draw to a greater extent on industries employing relatively more full-time workers (e.g., manufacturing).

The Multiplier Effect

A more comprehensive estimate of the number of jobs created by a particular type of economic activity has three components:

- the number of jobs directly attributable to the activity,
- the number of jobs indirectly attributable to the activity, and
- the number of jobs induced throughout the economy as a result of the activity.

Induced jobs are those dependent upon the purchases of persons in direct and indirect jobs. For example, workers who are directly or indirectly employed as the result of a highway construction program might spend some portion of their wages in their communities at grocery stores, auto repair shops, and movie theaters.

Estimates of induced jobs or the multiplier are considered tenuous. To calculate the multiplier effect, one must estimate how much of the additional money earned by directly and indirectly employed workers will likely be spent versus saved. The actual number of jobs created by this added spending will further depend on economic conditions (e.g., the availability of labor, the inflation rate). As a result, there are widely varying estimates of the multiplier effect and those job creation studies that include induced employment utilize different multipliers.

Job Estimates and Construction Spending

The FederalHighway Administration

Perhaps the most widely known estimate of the employment impact of federal spending on our nation's roads comes from the Federal Highway Administration (FHWA). Although the FHWA twice updated its 1997 analysis, which estimated that $1 billion of federal-aid highway expenditures plus a $250 million state match supported 47,575 jobs, some proponents of stimulating job growth through increased federal spending on infrastructure continue to use this figure. The most recent update by the FHWA to 2007 indicates that a $1.25 billion expenditure on highway construction consisting of $1 billion from the federal government and $250 million from state government could support 34,779 jobs. If a state match is not required, "then $1 billion in Federal funds supports 27,800 jobs."[6] The jobs number has decreased over time in part because of increases in the price of inputs, such as asphalt and diesel fuel.

The FHWA breaks down the estimate of 27,822 jobs per billion dollars of federal spending on highways as follows:

- 9,536 construction-oriented jobs (i.e., jobs at construction companies working on the projects and at businesses that provide direct inputs to the projects such as asphalt, concrete, and guard rails);
- 4,324 jobs in supporting industries (i.e., employment at firms that provide inputs to the industries directly providing the materials and equipment utilized in highway construction such as producers of sheet metal who supply the manufacturers of guard rails); and
- 13,962 induced jobs (i.e., jobs throughout the economy dependent upon consumer expenditures from the wages of workers in "construction-oriented" and "industry-supporting" jobs).

Thus, induced jobs account for one-half of the total estimate.

The FHWA notes one caveat about I-O analysis in addition to those mentioned above; that is, the job estimate "utilizes the national average mix of construction materials and labor inputs. Specific projects and local utilization ratios will alter the estimated number of jobs supported."[7] For example, a different combination of materials and number of workers might be required for road resurfacing projects compared to bridge building or commuter rail projects.

The FHWA also states that

> [t]he employment figures have recently been used as a justification for including highway spending in an economic stimulus package. But with the exception of short-term resurfacing and preservation projects, highway funds spend out slowly, with only 27% of a project, on average, outlaying in the first year.[8]

BLS EmploymentRequirements Table

In recognition of the fact that "people want to assess the impact on employment of different policies or actions," the U.S. Bureau of Labor Statistics (BLS) makes available electronically free-of-charge to the public the employment requirements tables it develops as part of its employment projections program.[9] I-O and employment requirements tables developed and utilized by others often are proprietary and not made widely available.

The employment requirements tables are based on the official I-O tables for the nation that the U.S. Bureau of Economic Analysis (BEA) develops every five years. BLS takes the latest national I-O table available from BEA—in this case, 1997—and updates it to reflect more recent production and distribution technologies. It then utilizes the updated I-O table and recent labor productivity data to develop an employment requirements table. The employment requirements table referenced in this chapter reflects 2006 technologies of production and distribution as well as labor productivity. It is the table that was available in late 2008 when this chapter was first released.[10]

The BLS employment requirements table provides information for the construction industry as a whole. The construction industry, according to the North American Industry Classification System, is composed of three major subdivisions:

- construction of buildings (residential and nonresidential),

- heavy and civil engineering construction (highway, street, and bridge construction; utility system construction; construction of flood control structures, dams, and hydroelectric power generation facilities), and
- specialty trade contractors (foundation, structure, and building exterior contractors; building equipment contractors; building finishing contractors).

Some 11,768 jobs are directly and indirectly dependent upon $1 billion of spending on construction. A majority of the jobs are in the construction industry itself (i.e., 6,925 direct jobs).

The figure from the BLS employment requirements table for construction expenditures (11,768) is somewhat lower than the direct and indirect jobs figure for highway expenditures from the FHWA (13,860). Potential explanations for the disparity include differences in industry definition, data sources, method of updating the model, and time period.

The employment requirements available from BLS do not break out other types of construction that have been discussed as part of a federal job creation package (e.g., public school construction). BLS formerly conducted surveys to estimate full-time year-long employment associated with a variety of different construction activities, including new schools, hospitals, water and sewer facilities, roads, mass transit, and maintenance and repair construction. The survey information was last updated a few decades ago, however.

BEA'sRegional Input-Output Modeling System (RIMS II)

From its Regional Input-Output Modeling System (RIMS II), the BEA produces estimates by geographic area of the employment, earnings, and output dependent on additional spending in hundreds of different industries. [11] For a fee to most parties, BEA utilizes either the 1997 benchmark I-O for the nation or the 2006 annual I-O for the nation adjusted by 2006 data from its regional economic accounts to provide these estimates at the subnational level.[12]

As shown in Table 1, the number of jobs directly and indirectly supported by an expenditure of $1 billion in the construction industry in a given state ranges widely. The main reason for the disparity in job creation estimates is that each state has a different mix of industries within its borders. As a consequence, one state varies from the next in its capacity to supply all the intermediate goods needed to carry out construction projects. A secondary explanation is that earnings vary by state.

Table 1. Number of Direct and Indirect Jobs by State Dependent on an Expenditure of $1 Billion in the Construction Industry

State	Number of Jobs	State	Number of Jobs
Alabama	15,851	Montana	16,127
Alaska	11,009	Nebraska	13,946
Arizona	12,238	Nevada	11,459
Arkansas	15,306	New Hampshire	12,374
California	12,289	New Jersey	11,118
Colorado	12,575	New Mexico	14,279
Connecticut	10,709	New York	10,106
Delaware	9,518	North Carolina	15,555
District of Columbia	1,874	North Dakota	13,500
Florida	13,127	Ohio	14,391
Georgia	14,224	Oklahoma	16,232
Hawaii	11,614	Oregon	13,184
Idaho	15,860	Pennsylvania	12,390
Illinois	11,916	Rhode Island	10,767
Indiana	13,747	South Carolina	15,319
Iowa	14,330	South Dakota	15,316
Kansas	13,625	Tennessee	14,556
Kentucky	15,039	Texas	12,985
Louisiana	13,731	Utah	14,692
Maine	15,988	Vermont	14,883
Maryland	10,687	Virginia	12,085
Massachusetts	10,714	Washington	12,171
Michigan	13,354	West Virginia	13,834
Minnesota	12,998	Wisconsin	13,673
Mississippi	15,357	Wyoming	13,091
Missouri	13,241	United States	14,315

Source: Prepared by CRS from RIMS II estimates supplied by the BEA Regional Product Division in 2008.

Job Estimates and Green Infrastructure Spending

Estimating the number of jobs dependent upon green infrastructure activities presents a greater challenge than estimates related to infrastructure projects as traditionally defined. The basis for most data collection by U.S. statistical agencies is the North American Industry Classification System (NAICS). It currently does not identify separately so-called green industries (e.g., those that utilize renewable resources to produce their outputs, those that manufacture goods which minimize energy use). For example, the NAICS disaggregates the electric utility industry into hydroelectric, fossil fuel, nuclear, and other power generation, transmission, and distribution. Such renewable sources of energy production as wind, solar, and biomass are not uniquely recognized; they are included in the "other" category. If harnessing the wind to produce electricity and plant material to produce biofuel requires a substantially different mix of inputs than relying on coal and gasoline, for example, the conventional I-O model does not seem well- suited as a basis for estimating the number of jobs supported by these green activities. Similarly, within NAICS, the construction industry does not have a unique category for retrofitting (e.g., installing additional insulation, fluorescent lighting, or energy-efficient heating and air- conditioning systems). Retrofitting likely requires a combination of inputs from supplier industries that differs from the mix for the top-to-bottom construction of buildings, once again making use of conventional I-O models problematic.

This recognized difficulty generally is either not mentioned, or how it is dealt with is not described, in the analyses of green job creation. One study, commissioned by the Center for American Progress and discussed in more detail below, does address the problem. The researchers explain that because "the U.S. government surveys and accounts that are used to construct the input-output tables do not specifically recognize wind, solar, biomass, building retrofitting, or new mass transit as industries in their own right," they created synthetic industries by combining parts of industries for which data are available. The researchers provided an example in the case of the biomass "industry:" they constructed it by combining farming, forestry, wood products, and refining industries; then they "assigned relative weights to each of these industries in terms of their contributions to producing biomass products."[13]

Further complicating the matter is the context and manner in which estimates of green jobs generally are presented. Studies often develop employment projections based on differing sets of assumptions and time horizons. For example, the number of direct and indirect jobs some 10 or more years in the future supported by an assumed increase in the demand for energy that is met by an assumed shift during the projection period from coal to wind and geothermal power generation. Some reports also include induced employment, but this is not always made clear. In addition, some analyses relate to a particular state. Their results may not be generalizeable to other areas because state economy's have different mixes of industries and may not be able to provide any or all of the inputs for a particular green output. Additionally, the assumptions and methodologies underlying the job creation estimates often are not clearly articulated, which makes thoughtful review of the results very difficult.

It should be noted that many of the studies by green economy proponents that were available when Congress was crafting stimulus legislation had not been conceived for the purpose of quickly stabilizing or increasing the number of jobs in the nation or in industries particularly hard hit by the recession. Job creation estimates from two organizations that proposed broad-based green economy strategies intended in part to stimulate the deteriorating labor market are briefly described below.

> The September 2008 report, *Green Recovery: A Program to Create Jobs and Start Building a Low-Carbon Economy*, was commissioned by the Center for American Progress (a research and educational institute). It represents an acceleration of a 10-year program included in a 2007 report (*Capturing the Energy Opportunity: Creating a Low-Carbon Economy*). The 2008 report's authors at the Department of Economics and Political Economy Research Institute (University of Massachusetts-Amherst), who relied on I-O analysis, estimate that almost 2 million jobs (935,200 direct jobs, 586,000 indirect jobs, and 496,000 induced jobs) could be created or preserved by a two-year $100 billion "green economic recovery program." Of the $100 billion total, $46 billion would be in the form of federal spending for such activities as public building retrofits, mass transit and freight rail expansion, and smart electrical grid development. Much of the remainder would be in the form of tax credits to encourage businesses and homeowners to retrofit commercial and residential buildings. The authors acknowledge that not all of the green activities can contribute equally to a short-term green economic recovery program. Some ... strategies are clearly capable of delivering within a year, while others will require as long as two years to be implemented.[14]

- In December 2008, the Apollo Alliance (a coalition of labor, environmental, business and community leaders) proposed *The Apollo Economic Recovery Act.*

  It is an initial step toward achievement of a 10-year $500 billion program to create 5 million green-collar jobs, which had been released in September 2008. The new initiative calls for federal spending of about $50 billion to create or maintain more than 650,000 direct jobs and 1.3 million indirect jobs. The derivation of these job creation figures is not always clear, appearing to rely much of the time on spending-to-jobs relationships estimated by other organizations. The proposed allocation of federal funds and associated job estimates include $10 billion to improve the efficiency and reliability of the electric transmission grid (131,000 direct and indirect jobs), $8 billion to repair roads and bridges (278,000 direct and indirect jobs), and $8 billion to encourage localities to replace aging buses and trains with U.S.-made clean-energy vehicles (37,600 direct jobs in vehicle manufacturing and 167,000 indirect jobs).

MEASURING JOBS SUPPORTED BY SPENDING PROVISIONS IN THE AMERICAN RECOVERY AND REINVESTMENT ACT

While crafting the American Recovery and Reinvestment Act (ARRA), Congress was concerned about timely tracking of the number of jobs whose creation or maintenance results from the legislation. The 111th Congress therefore addressed this matter in bill language much more than prior Congresses had in countercyclical job creation legislation.

Job Reporting by Recipients of ARRA Appropriations

At Title XV—Accountability and Transparency of Division A—Appropriations Provisions, P.L. 111-5 requires entities that receive ARRA appropriations from federal agencies (e.g., grant, loan, or contract recipients; states) to include in their quarterly reports to the agencies estimates of the number of direct jobs created and retained by infrastructure projects, for example.[15] Recipients of recovery funds were required to make their first submission of the required information in October 2009. Federal agencies are required to post the contents of these and subsequent reports on websites 30 days after the end of each calendar quarter. The Office of Management and Budget (OMB) was directed to provide guidance to help recipients prepare the reports, including the development of job estimates. The act further charged the Congressional Budget Office (CBO) and the Government Accountability

Office (GAO) with commenting on the job estimates contained in the reports within 45 days after their submission to federal agencies.

Based on the self-reporting of recipients of ARRA appropriations, 640,329 jobs were saved or retained through September 30, 2009. Because the notion of a retained (saved) job caused consternation in some quarters, the OMB revised its guidance issued in June 2009. According to that guidance, upon which the aforementioned job figure was based, Congress' reference in ARRA to a job retained meant "an existing position that would not have been continued to be filled were it not for Recovery Act funding."[16] In response to feedback from the General Accountability Office, among others, the OMB revised its guidance on jobs saved so that recipients no longer will have "to make a subjective judgment on whether a given job would have existed were it not for the Recovery Act. The updated guidance [issued in December 2009] ... defines jobs created or retained as those funded ... by the Recovery Act."[17] Based on this definition, recipients reported that 608,317 jobs were funded by ARRA in the fourth quarter of 2009. Another 682,226 jobs were created or saved at ARRA recipients in the first quarter of 2010.

Job Estimation by the Council of Economic Advisers

Title XV of P.L. 111-5 additionally tasked the Council of Economic Advisers (CEA) with submitting quarterly reports to the Committees on Appropriations on the effect of ARRAprovisions on employment and other economic indicators. The CEA's mandate thus extends well beyond the above-described reporting requirements, which apply only to $271 billion in direct government investment spending out of a total of $787 billion.[18]

The first quarterly report of the CEA was issued in September 2009. Based on two different estimating procedures, it found that ARRA might have added some one million jobs to employer payrolls in August 2009 compared to what employment would have been in the absence of the legislation.[19]

As noted above, CBO was charged in ARRA with commenting on the number of jobs created or saved as a result of direct government purchases of goods and services, grants and loans to private entities, and grants to states and localities. Although it did so in *Estimated Impact of the American Recovery and Reinvestment Act on Employment and Economic Output as of September 2009*, CBO went further to provide a broader estimate than can be gleaned from the reports of primary and secondary recipients of more than $25,000 from appropriations in ARRA; it is an estimate more comparable to that of the

CEA. Based upon information provided by macroeconomic models and historical relationships, CBO estimated that ARRA's tax cuts and outlay increases that occurred through September 2009 increased the number of people employed by between 600,000 and 1.6 million compared to the employment level without the law. The CEA's estimate of about 1 million additional jobs as of August 2009, discussed in the preceding paragraph, falls within the range estimated by CBO as of the third quarter of 2009.

In its second quarterly report, released in January 2010, the CEA estimated the effect of ARRA on employment through December 2009. It found that the stimulus law might have raised year-end employment by about 1.7–2.0 million jobs above what it otherwise would have been.[20] Similarly, CBO estimated in its report covering the fourth quarter of 2009 that ARRA's policies might have increased the number of people employed by 1.0–2.1 million.[21]

The CEA's third quarterly report, released in April 2010, showed ARRA's employment effect through March 2010. It estimated that the law might have raised employment by 2.2–2.8 million jobs above what it otherwise would have been as of the first quarter of 2010.[22] Similarly, CBO estimated in its report covering the first quarter of 2010 that ARRA's policies might have increased the number of people employed by 1.2–2.8 million.[23]

End Notes

[1] CRS Report R40798, *Unemployment and Employment Trends Before and After the End of Recessions*, by Linda Levine.

[2] CRS Report 92-939, *Countercyclical Job Creation Programs*, by Linda Levine.

[3] Related jobs include, for example, those in industries that manufacture wind turbines and install thermal-pane windows.

[4] Small differences in the total number of jobs could occur at the same spending levels if the economic activities to (from) which funds were being shifted were more (less) capital-intensive, for example.

[5] Another basis for estimating the impact of policy and other changes on the economy is conducting surveys. According to the U.S. Bureau of Economic Analysis (BEA), the advantage of the I-O approach to making impact estimates is the accessibility of the data sources required to develop the I-O model.

[6] U.S. Department of Transportation, Federal Highway Administration, *Employment Impacts of Highway Infrastructure Investment.* Available from author upon request.

[7] Ibid.

[8] Ibid.

[9] U.S. Bureau of Labor Statistics, Layout and Description for 201-order Employment Requirements Tables, Washington, DC, December 2007, p. 3, *http://stats.bls.gov /emp/empind4.htm.*

[10] BLS in late 2009 released an employment requirements table updated to reflect 2008 technologies of production and distribution as well as labor productivity. It is available at http://stats.bls.gov/emp/ep_data_emp_requirements.htm.

[11] For additional information on RIMS II see BEA, *Regional Multipliers: A User Handbook for the Regional Input- Output Modeling System*, *http://www.bea.gov/scb/pdf /regional/perinc/meth/rims2.pdf.*

[12] More specific detail by industry is available from the 1997 benchmark I-O than from the annual I-O. Therefore, Table 1 (Number of Direct and Indirect Jobs Per $1 Million of Output Produced by the Water, Sewage and Other Systems Industry) in CRS Report R40 107, *The Role of Public Works Infrastructure in Economic Stimulus*, was drawn from the 1997 benchmark I-O because the 2006 annual I-O provides data only for the utilities industry as a whole.

[13] Robert Pollin, Heidi Garrett-Peltier, and James Heintz, et al., *Green Recovery: A Program to Create Good Jobs and Start Building a Low-Carbon Economy*, Center for American Progress, Washington, DC, September 2008, p. 20, http://www.americanprogress.org.

[14] Robert Pollin, Heidi Garrett-Peltier, and James Heintz, et al., *Green Recovery: A Program to Create Good Jobs and Start Building a Low-Carbon Economy*, Center for American Progress, Washington, DC, September 2008, p. 5, http://www.americanprogress.org.

[15] Recipients of ARRA funds awarded to the Department of Transportation (DOT) are subject to Section 1512's job reporting requirement. Separately, at Section 1201, Congress required the DOT to estimate the direct, indirect, and total jobs created by transportation projects funded under ARRA. The DOT estimates thus are akin to the estimates for the entire bill that the CEA produces.

[16] OMB, *Implementing Guidance for the Reports on Use of Funds Pursuant to the American Recovery and Reinvestment Act*, M-09-21, June 22, 2009, available at http://www.whitehouse.gov/omb/assets m09-21.pdf.

[17] OMB, *Updated Guidance on the American Recovery and Reinvestment Act—Data Quality, Non-Reporting Recipients, and Reporting of Job Estimates*, M-10-08, December 18, 2009. See Part 2 of http://www.recovery.gov/ FAQ/recipient/Documents/m10-08%20Updated% 20Guidance%20121 82009.pdf.

[18] The remaining ARRA funds fall into five categories: individual income tax cuts, a patch for the alternative minimum tax, investment incentives, aid to people directly hurt by the recession (e.g., unemployment insurance), and fiscal relief for state governments.

[19] Council of Economic Advisers, *The Economic Impact of the American Recovery and Reinvestment Act of 2009, First Quarterly Report,* September 10, 2009.

[20] Council of Economic Advisers, *The Economic Impact of the American Recovery and Reinvestment Act of 2009, Second Quarterly Report*, January 13, 2010.

[21] Congressional Budget Office, *Estimated Impact of the American Recovery and Reinvestment Act on Employment and Economic Output From October 2009 Through December 2009*, February 2010.

[22] Council of Economic Advisers, *The Economic Impact of the American Recovery and Reinvestment Act of 2009, Third Quarterly Report*, April 14, 2010.

[23] Congressional Budget Office, *Estimated Impact of the American Recovery and Reinvestment Act on Employment and Economic Output From January 2010 Through March 2010*, May 2010.

In: Recession, Depression, and Unemployment ISBN: 978-1-61761-508-5
Editors: Daniel A. García

Chapter 3

UNEMPLOYMENT AND EMPLOYMENT TRENDS BEFORE AND AFTER THE END OF RECESSIONS

Linda Levine

The economy has been showing signs that the worst of the recession that began in December 2007 may be over.[1] But, one economic indicator that is very visible in people's daily lives—the unemployment rate—continues to rise. With the unemployment rate at 9.7% in August 2009,[2] those still employed or able to find jobs 20 months into the recession are quite likely to know personally others who have been less fortunate. In addition, the still high and rising percentage of workers without jobs for so long that their eligibility for unemployment benefits soon might be exhausted[3] is of concern to Members of Congress who have extended benefit duration on more than one occasion since the recession's onset.[4] And, there is consternation in some quarters that firms thus far have not begun to hire or recall from layoff more workers than leave their employ despite enactment in February 2009 of the American Recovery and Reinvestment Act (P.L. 111-5).

This chapter addresses the question of when one might reasonably expect to see sustained improvement in the unemployment rate and a steady resumption of job growth. It first provides an explanation of

- why the unemployment rate is unlikely to begin trending downward before the end of 2009, and
- why the number of jobs is unlikely to start trending upward until 2010 arrives.

The report then analyzes the trend in the unemployment rate and jobs data before and after the bottom of prior business cycles to confirm these statements.

Explanation of Trends in Unemployment and Jobs around the Bottom of the Business Cycle

A few definitions are called for before proceeding with the explanation. To begin with, the official definition of the unemployment rate prescribed by the U.S. Bureau of Labor Statistics (BLS) is the percentage of persons in the civilian labor force age 16 and older who are unemployed. The labor force, in turn, is defined as the number of employed and unemployed individuals in the civilian noninstitutional population age 16 and older. Lastly, unemployment is defined as the number of people who actively searched for work in the four weeks before the week in which the Census Bureau administers the Current Population Survey to members of households. Mathematically, the unemployment rate is expressed as:

$$\frac{\text{the number of unemployed persons}}{\text{the number of unemployed and employed persons}}$$

The unemployment rate consequently may move up or down depending not just on a change in the number of workers who lack jobs (the numerator) but also on a change in the number of individuals participating in the labor force (the denominator). The size of the labor force may decrease during a recession in part because unemployed workers who give up searching for jobs out of discouragement over their reemployment prospects cease to be included. Conversely, the number of labor force participants may increase during a recession if people see signs the economy is improving and think it again worthwhile to look for work.[5] If hiring does not keep pace with persons (re)entering the labor force, however, the unemployment rate will rise in the face of otherwise good economic news. The unemployment rate thus is called a lagging economic indicator: it typically improves only after other indicators have signaled an impending recovery and actually may rise for some time after a recession's end.

Firms usually are reluctant to add workers to their payrolls until convinced that the economy will continue growing (i.e., gross domestic product, GDP, will keep increasing). Before employers are fairly certain that the increase in demand for their goods and services will continue, they are likely to boost production by restoring the hours of those currently in their employ and by having employees work overtime rather than by hiring new workers or recalling laid off workers.[6] As a result, job growth may not occur immediately upon the economy showing signs of a turnaround.[7]

The source of jobs data that labor market analysts generally utilize is the Current Employment Statistics program. In its establishment survey, BLS queries nonfarm employers each month about the number of jobs (employees) on their payrolls. Employers are considered to be a more accurate source for this information compared to the members of households who respond to the Current Population Survey, from which the unemployment rate and most demographic information on workers is derived. In addition, the Business Cycle Dating Committee appears to rely chiefly on changes in both national output (GDP) and employment trends from the establishment survey to determine the official beginning and end of recessions.

TRENDS IN UNEMPLOYMENT AND JOBS BEFORE AND AFTER THE END OF PRIOR RECESSIONS

The U.S. economy experienced 10 recessions since World War II, excluding the latest, which began in December 2007. They varied greatly in severity, as measured by the extent of decline in GDP and their duration.[8]But, without exception, the unemployment rate kept increasing until or after each recession had ended. (See Table 1.)

The unemployment rate peaked at the bottom of the business cycle in three instances: at 7.9% in October 1949, at 7.8% in July 1980, and at 10.8% in November 1982. In the remaining seven recessions, the unemployment rate did not peak until after they had ended. Four times the unemployment rate kept climbing for only a few months into the economic recovery: four months after the July 1953-May 1954 recession ended, three months after the August 1957-

April 1958 recession and the April 1960-February 1961 recession ended, and two months after the November 1973-March 1975 recession ended.

In contrast, the unemployment rate did not peak until well into the economic recovery in three instances. The unemployment rate kept rising for nine months after the end of the December 1969-November 1970 recession, 15 months after the end of the July 1990-March 1991 recession, and 18 months after the end of the March-November 2001 recession.

Like the unemployment rate, the employment data generally fit the posited trend of no job growth before 2010. As shown in Figure 1, a sustained period of job growth failed to ensue until after the end of all 10 recessions. In only one of those instances—the very short January-July 1980 recession—did the employment level immediately begin trending upward.

In the other nine cases, the number of jobs on employer payrolls fluctuated for months after the recession's end. Sustained job growth occurred within three to five months of the start of seven recoveries. In sharp contrast, steady job growth did not commence until March 1992—12 months after the July 1990-March 1991 recession ended; and not until September 2003—22 months after the March-November 2001 recession ended. The very delayed improvement in the labor market following the two recessions meant that pre-recession levels of employment were not attained until early 1993, in the case of the 1990-1991 recession, and until early 2005, in the case of the 2001 recession. As a result, the two most recent rebounds of the economy commonly are referred to as jobless recoveries.[9]

Some observers think that a jobless recovery may follow the latest recession, at least in part because the sluggishness of the recoveries from the 1990-1991 and 2001 recessions suggests the economy somehow may have changed fundamentally in recent decades.[10] Other analysts instead look for guidance about the nature of the upcoming recovery in the experience after the 1973- 1975 and 1981-1982 recessions, because they too were deep and long.[11] As discussed previously in this chapter, the recoveries in the labor market that followed the two deep recessions were comparatively swift. The unemployment rate continued to rise for only two months after the end of the 1973-1975 recession before steadily improving. In the case of the 1981-1982 recession, the peak unemployment rate reached at its end remained the same in the following month and declined thereafter. With respect to sustained job growth, it took hold only four months into both recoveries (see Figure 1).

Table 1 . The Unemployment Rate at a Recession's End and at the Rate's Peak

Dates of Business Cycle Peak and Trough	Unemployment Rate at Trough	Peak Unemployment Rate	
		Level	Date
Nov. 1948 - Oct. 1949	7.9%	7.9%	Oct. 1949
July 1953 - May 1954	5.9%	6.1%	Sept. 1954
Aug. 1957 - Apr. 1958	7.4%	7.5%	July 1958
Apr. 1960 - Feb. 1961	6.9%	7.1%	May 1961
Dec. 1969 - Nov. 1970	5.9%	6.1%	Aug. 1971
Nov. 1973 - Mar. 1975	8.6%	9.0%	May 1975
Jan. 1980 - July 1980	7.8%	7.8%	July 1980
July 1981 - Nov. 1982	10.8%	10.8%	Nov. 1982
July 1990 - Mar. 1991	6.8%	7.8%	June 1992
Mar. 2001 - Nov. 2001	5.5%	6.3%	July 2003

Source: Created by the Congressional Research Service from the Bureau of Labor Statistics' unemployment rate series and from the Business Cycle Dating Committee's start and end points of recessions.

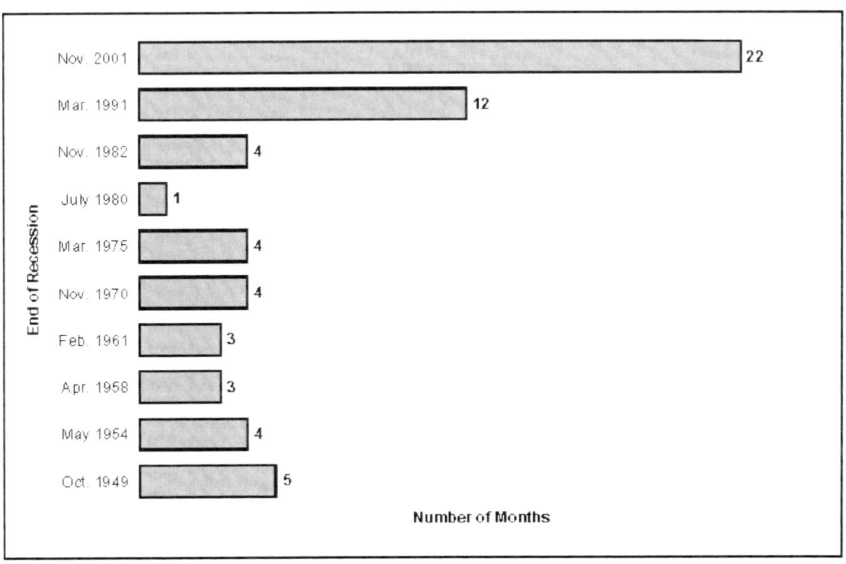

Source: Created by the Congressional Research Service from the Bureau of Labor Statistics jobs data and Business Cycle Dating Committee for end date of recessions.

Figure 1. Number of Months into Recovery When Sustained Job Growth Began.

End Notes

[1] "Leading Index Increases for the Fourth Month, Suggest Recovery Likely Soon," *Daily Labor Report*, August 21, 2009.

[2] Bureau of Labor Statistics, *The Employment Situation*, news release, September 4, 2009.

[3] In August 2009, workers unemployed for at least six months accounted for one in every three unemployed persons according to BLS data. Their prevalence is up from fewer than one in five at the recession's onset in December 2007.

[4] CRS Report RS22915, *Temporary Extension of Unemployment Benefits: Emergency Unemployment Compensation (EUC08)*, by Julie M. Whittaker and Alison M. Shelton.

[5] The number of discouraged workers—that is, persons not in the labor force who are available to take a job now but are not currently looking because they think no work is available for them—rose from fewer than 400,000 at the recession's outset to 758,000 in August 2009, according to BLS data. This figure provides a suggestion of the extent to which the labor force might increase once people sense an economic turnaround is underway. (In August 2009, there were 154,577,000 (employed and unemployed) persons in the labor force.)

[6] The average workweek of production and nonsupervisory workers on nonfarm employer payrolls dropped from 33.8 hours in December 2007, to 33.1 hours in August 2009, according to BLS data. The decrease was deeper for production workers in manufacturing industries where average hours worked fell from 41.2 to 39.8; included in these totals are overtime hours, which fell from 4.1 to 2.9. The figures provide a suggestion of the room employers have to increase output before hiring new workers.

[7] Wherever the phrase "job growth" appears in this chapter it refers to the net change in employment over time (i.e., the difference between the number of jobs on employer payrolls in one time period compared to another).

[8] CRS Report R40198, *U.S. Economy in Recession: Similarities To and Differences From the Past*, by Marc Labonte. (Hereafter referred to as CRS Report R40 198, *U.S. Economy in Recession.*)

[9] CRS Report RL32047, *The "Jobless Recovery" From the 2001 Recession: A Comparison to Earlier Recoveries and Possible Explanations*, by Marc Labonte and Linda Levine.

[10] During and shortly after the sluggish recovery from the 2001 recession, a few economists examined whether changes in the industrial structure of the economy (e.g., from manufacturing and toward health care services) resulted in an unusually large number of workers who lost jobs having to undertake the time-consuming process of searching for new jobs in other industries rather than being recalled from temporary layoffs by their former employers. While Erica L. Groshen and Simon Potter ("Has Structural Change Contributed to a Jobless Recovery?" *Current Issues in Economics and Finance*, vol. 9, no. 8, Federal Reserve Bank of New York, August 2003) estimated that structural change was a cause of the jobless recovery, the findings of Daniel Aaronson, Ellen R. Rissman, and Daniel G. Sullivan ("Can Sectoral Reallocation Explain the Jobless Recovery?" *Economic Perspectives*, Federal Reserve Bank of Chicago, 2nd quarter 2004)—which are based on a different measure of employment reallocation across industries—do not support the other study's results. More recently, Jacob Funk Kirkegaard ("Structural and Cyclical Trends in Net Employment over US Business Cycles, 1949-2009: Implications for the Next Recovery and Beyond," Peterson Institute for International Economics Working Paper series, August 2009) expanded on the methodology of Groshen and Potter to study the effect on employment trends during postwar recessions of cyclical and structural changes in the economy. He estimates that structural employment declines have accelerated in manufacturing industries and recently, in segments of financial activities (e.g., securities, commodities contracts) while structural employment gains have become increasingly concentrated in health care, education, and food services. From these results, Kirkegaard suggests that many of those who lost jobs during the current recession will have to find

positions in industries different from those in which they worked previously. He further notes that although the methodology of the analysis "does not necessarily point in the short term to a very weak or a jobless recovery, ... [it does] suggest that once the immediate job-creating effects of the unprecedented fiscal stimulus spending, zero interest rate policy, and cyclical business inventory and real estate investments recede, the US labor market is in for a long, hard slog."

[11] CRS Report R40 198, *U.S. Economy in Recession.*

In: Recession, Depression, and Unemployment ISBN: 978-1-61761-508-5
Editors: Daniel A. García

Chapter 4

EXTENDING UNEMPLOYMENT COMPENSATION BENEFITS DURING RECESSIONS

Julie M. Whittaker

SUMMARY

This chapter describes the history of temporary federal extensions to unemployment benefits from 1980 to the present. Among these extensions is the Emergency Unemployment Compensation (EUC08) program created by P.L. 110-252 (amended by P.L. 110-449 and P.L. 111-5). It also provides information on the legislative timing of those temporary programs. Additionally, the report includes information on economic recessions and possible triggers for the extension of unemployment benefits.

This chapter contains four sections. The first section provides background information on unemployment compensation (UC) benefits. It also provides a brief summary of UC benefit exhaustion and how exhaustion rates are related to the business cycle.

The second section provides the definition of a recession as well as the determination process for declaring a recession. It also provides information on the timing of all recessions since 1980.

The third section summarizes the legislative history of federal extensions of unemployment benefits. It includes information on the permanently authorized extended benefit (EB) program as well as information on temporary unemployment benefit extensions. It also includes a brief discussion on the role of extended unemployment benefits as part of an economic stimulus package.

The fourth section provides figures examining of the timing of recessions and statistics that may be considered for determining extending unemployment benefits.

The Appendix contains tables summarizing the legislative history of federal extensions of unemployment benefits.

Unemployment Compensation and Exhaustion of Benefits

The cornerstone of an unemployed worker's income support is the joint federal-state Unemployment Compensation (UC)[1] program, which may provide income support through the payment of UC benefits. The underlying framework of the UC system is contained in the Social Security Act. Title III of the act authorizes grants to states for the administration of state UC laws, Title IX authorizes the various components of the federal Unemployment Trust Fund (UTF), and Title XII authorizes advances or loans to insolvent state UC programs. UC is financed by federal taxes under the Federal Unemployment Tax Act (FUTA) and by state payroll taxes under the State Unemployment Tax Acts (SUTA).

The federal government funds federal and state UC program administration, the federal share (50%) of Extended Benefit (EB) payments, 100% of the Emergency Unemployment Compensation (EUC08) program, and federal loans to insolvent state UC programs. States fund regular state UC benefits and the state share (5 0%) of EB payments. The American recovery and Reinvestment Act of 2009 (P.L. 111-5) temporarily provides for 100% federal funding of EB through December 2009.

In FY2008, the states received an estimated $2.73 billion from the federal government for the administration of their regular UC programs and for the administration of the federal Emergency Unemployment Compensation (EUC08) program. In FY2008, states spent an estimated $38.1 billion on regular UC benefits and $4.1 million on EB payments.

UC Benefits and Duration

Workers who lose their jobs face serious long-term economic implications. In general, they face a substantially reduced probability of full-time employment and an increased probability of part- time employment. Those workers who find new full-time employment on average experience significantly decreased earnings relative to what they earned before they lost employment.

The UC program pays benefits to workers in covered employment who become involuntarily unemployed for economic reasons and meet state-established eligibility rules. The UC program generally does not provide UC benefits to the self-employed, to those who are unable to work, or to those who do not have a recent earnings history. States usually disqualify claimants who lost their jobs because of inability to work or unavailability for work, who voluntarily quit without good cause, who were discharged for job-related misconduct, or who refused suitable work without good cause.

This temporary unemployment insurance benefit is designed to be sufficient to meet an unemployed worker's basic obligations until the worker finds a new position. Generally, benefits are based on wages for covered work over a 12-month period. The entitlement formula varies by state, typically requiring a substantial work history and replacing between 50%-80% of workers' wages. Generally, benefits are capped at a percentage of the average wage for workers in the state, which generally lowers the average replacement rate for all worker nationwide to less than 50% (25% in the 4th quarter of 2008). Weekly maximums in January 2009 ranged from $230 (Mississippi) to $600 (Massachusetts) and, in states that provide dependent's allowances, up to $942 (Massachusetts). In the fourth quarter of CY2008, the average weekly benefit was $300. Benefits are available for up to 26 weeks (28 weeks in Montana and 30 weeks in Massachusetts). The average regular UC benefit duration in fourth quarter of CY2008 was 14.9 weeks. In FY2008, the ratio of unemployed workers who receive benefits to all those who are unemployed ranges from a low of 0.19 (South Dakota) to a high of 0.68 (Idaho). In FY2008, 40% of all U.S. unemployed workers received UC benefits.

Generally the UC recipency rate (the ratio of unemployed receiving UC benefits to all unemployed) rises during economic recessions (as workers with strong labor market experience are laid-off) and falls during economic expansions (as new entrants to the labor market begin to comprise a greater proportion of the unemployed).[2]

Generosity of UnemploymentBenefits and Disincentives to FindWork

The difficulty in monitoring job search intensity creates the risk the unemployed will abuse a system designed to alleviate the worst financial aspects of job loss. Although UC benefits create a clear disincentive to find work quickly, this disincentive is balanced by a relatively low replacement rate of wages by UC benefits and a recognition that proper allocation of human resources and human capital requires adequate job search time.[3]

The job-search behavior of the unemployed can be influenced by changing the timing, generosity, and duration of UC benefits. Higher benefit levels and easier program requirements for benefits will cause recipients to be less willing to accept jobs and may alleviate some of the social stigma from being unemployed.[4] Thus, the availability of benefits may create a disincentive to search for and accept reemployment, increasing unemployment and unemployment duration.[5]

UC Benefit Exhaustion

The limited duration of UC benefits (generally 26 weeks) will result in some unemployed individuals exhausting their UC benefits before finding work or voluntarily leaving the labor force for other reasons such as retirement, disability, family care, or education. Empirical research suggests that workers who exhaust benefits search at similar or higher levels of intensity as those workers who do find employment before benefit exhaustion.[6] Most state UC programs attempt to identify potential benefit exhaustees through a profiling system. Workers who are identified as likely to become unemployed long-term are offered intensive employment services.[7]

Figure 1 displays the percent of UC beneficiaries both as a percent of all unemployed workers (the "recipiency rate") and as the number of UC benefitexhaustees since 1979. (Please note that Figure 1 uses different numerical scales for the recipiency rate and for the exhaustion rate. Because the correspondence between the two scales was determined by scaling size rather than by a particular economic correspondence, readers should not place any significance in the two lines crossing each other. The scale for the recipiency rate is located on the left-hand y-axis. The scale for the UC benefit exhaustees is located on the right-hand y-axis.)

The proportion of UC recipients who exhaust their benefits varies according to economic conditions, state benefit duration formulas, and the composition of the labor force. Some evidence suggests that an aging workforce may have increased the proportion of unemployed workers who are long-term unemployed; at the same time, this aging workforce may also have contributed to the decrease in the overall unemployment rate.[8]

RECESSIONS

Determination of a Recession

The National Bureau of Economic Research (NBER)—not the federal government—declares when a recession began.[9] A recession is a significant decline in economic activity spread across the economy, lasting more than a few months, normally visible in measures of real gross domestic product (GDP), real income, employment, industrial production, and wholesale-retail sales. [10] A recession begins just after the economy reaches a peak of activity and ends as the economy reaches its trough. Between a trough and a peak, the economy is in an expansion.

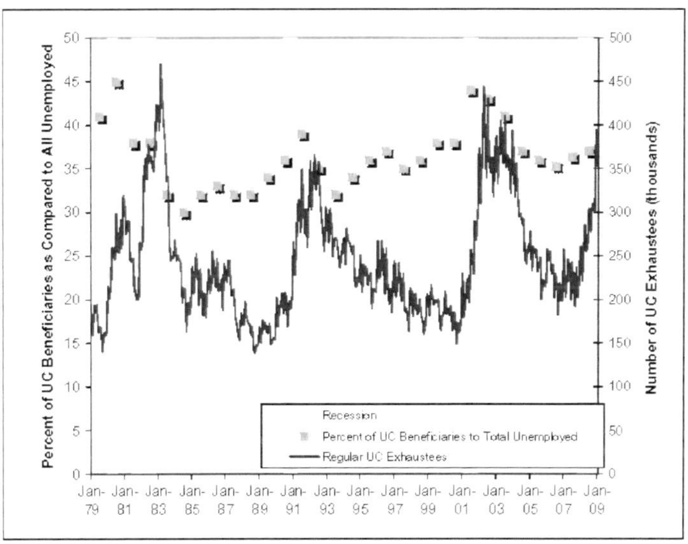

Source: Congressional Research Service. Data are from Department of Labor, Employment and Training Administration. *http://www.doleta.gov/unemploy/chartbook.cfm*

Figure 1. Economic Recessions, Percent of Regular UC Beneficiaries to All Unemployed, and UC Benefit Exhaustees, January 1979- January 2009.

CurrentRecessionBeganDecember 2007

The NBER maintains a time line of the U.S. business cycle. This chronology identifies the dates of peaks and troughs that frame economic recessions or expansions. According to NBER, a peak was reached in December 2007, marking the end of the expansion that began in November 2001 and thus marking the beginning of the current recession.

The most recent expansion lasted 73 months; the previous expansion of the 1990s lasted 120 months.

Recessionsfrom 1980 to Present

Since 1980 there have been five separate periods that the NBER has identified as recessions: January 1980-July 1980; July 1981-November 1982; July 1990-March 1991; March 2001- November 2001; and the ongoing December 2007 recession.

FEDERAL PROGRAMS OF EXTENDED UNEMPLOYMENT COMPENSATION

The Unemployment Compensation program's two main objectives are to provide temporary and partial wage replacement to involuntarily unemployed workers and to stabilize the economy during recessions.[11] These objectives are reflected in the current UC program's funding and benefit structure. When the economy grows, UC program revenue rises through increased tax revenues while UC program spending falls as fewer workers are unemployed and receive benefits. The effect of collecting more taxes while decreasing spending on benefits dampens demand in the economy. This also creates a surplus of funds or a "cushion" of available funds for the UC program to draw upon during a recession. In a recession, UC tax revenue falls and UC program spending rises as more workers lose their jobs and receive UC benefits. The increased amount of UC payments to unemployed workers dampens the economic effect of lost earnings by injecting additional funds into the economy.

In response to economic recessions, the federal government sometimes has augmented the regular UC benefit with both permanent (the EB program) and temporary extensions (including the EUC08 program) of the duration of unemployment benefits.

Extended Benefit (EB) Program (Determined at the State Level)

The Extended Benefit program was established by the Federal-State Extended Unemployment Compensation Act of 1970 (EUCA), P.L. 91-373 (26 U.S.C. 3304, note). EUCA may extend receipt of unemployment benefits (extended benefits) at the state level if certain economic situations exist within the state. The Omnibus Budget Reconciliation Act of 1981, P.L. 97-3 5, among other items, amended the EUCA to require that claimants have worked at least 20 weeks of full-time insured employment or the equivalent in insured wages.

The EB program is triggered when a state's insured unemployment rate (IUR)[12] or total unemployment rate (TUR)[13] reaches certain levels. All states must pay up to 13 weeks of EB if the IUR for the previous 13 weeks is at least 5% and is 120% of the average of the rates for the same 13-week period in each of the 2 previous years. There are two other optional thresholds that states may choose. (States may chose one, two, or neither of the additional options.) If the state has chosen the option, they would provide the following:

- Option 1: an additional 13 weeks of benefits if the state's IUR is at least 6%, regardless of previous years' averages.
- Option 2: an additional 13 weeks of benefits if the state's TUR is at least 6.5% and is at least 110% of the state's average TUR for the same 13-weeks in either of the previous two years; an additional 20 weeks of benefits if the TUR is at least 8% and is at least 110% of the state's average TUR for the same 13-weeks in either of the previous two years.

The EB program imposes additional restrictions on individual eligibility for benefits. It requires that a worker be actively searching and available for work. Furthermore, the worker may not receive benefits if the worker refused an offer of suitable work. Finally, claimants must have recorded least 20 weeks of full-time insured employment or the equivalent in insured wages during their base period (the four quarters of earnings used to determine UC benefit eligibility).

Methods for Determining 20 Weeks of Full-Time InsuredEmployment

States use one, two, or three different methods for determining an "equivalent" to 20 weeks of full-time insured employment. These methods are described in both law (Section 202(a)(5) of the EUCA) and regulation (20

CFR 615.4(b)). In practice, states that require any of these three requirements for receipt of regular UC benefits *and* do not allow for exceptions to those requirements do not need to establish that the worker met the 20 weeks full-time insured employment. [14] The three methods are listed below.

- earnings in the base period equal to at least 1.5 times the high-quarter wages; or
- earnings in the base period of at least 40 times the most recent weekly benefit amount, and if this alternative is adopted, it shall use the weekly benefit amount (including dependents' allowances) payable for a week of total unemployment (before any reduction because of earnings, pensions or other requirements) that applied to the most recent week of regular benefits; or
- earnings in the base period equal to at least 20 weeks of full-time insured employment, and if this alternative is adopted, the term "full-time" shall have the meaning provided by the state law.

The base period may be the regular base period or, if applicable in the state, the period may be the alternative base period or the extended base period if that determined the regular UC benefit.

EB Provisions in the American Recovery and ReinvestmentAct of 2009

The American Recovery and Reinvestment Act of 2009 (P.L. 111-5, also known as ARRA or the 2009 stimulus package) contains several provisions affecting unemployment benefits. Among these provisions was a temporary change increasing the federal share to 100% in the cost sharing agreement for EB through the end of 2009. (The permanent funding arrangement is 50% federal funding and 50% state funding.) ARRA also provides a supplemental $25 weekly benefit through December 2009 for recipients of unemployment benefits, including EB. Finally, ARRA also allows states, at their option, to temporarily change the eligibility requirements for the EB program in order to expand the number of persons eligible for EB benefits.[15]

Temporary Federal Extensions of Unemployment Benefits: Congressional Intervention in Recessions

During some economic recessions, Congress has created federal temporary programs of extended unemployment compensation. Congress acted eight times—in 1958, 1961, 1971, 1974, 1982, 1991, 2002, and 2008—to establish these temporary programs of extended UC benefits. These programs extended the time an individual might claim UC benefits (ranging from an additional 6 to 33 weeks) and had expiration dates. Some extensions took into account state economic conditions; many temporary programs considered the state's total TUR or the state's IUR or both.

Historically, these programs started operation after the trough of a recession had passed (i.e., after the recession had officially ended). This is due to several reasons. One cause is that NBER often announces that a recession has begun three or more months after what is later determined to be the official start. Another cause to this lag in response time is that often the severity of the recession and its impact on unemployment levels does not become apparent until several quarters after the recession begins.

The 1958 and the 1961 programs were proposed and enacted after the trough of those recessions but before the unemployment rate had peaked. The 1971 program was enacted after the end of the recession in November 1970. Both the 1974 and 1982 programs also became effective toward the end of those recessions. The 1991 program was enacted eight months after the 1990-1991 recession trough but eight months before the unemployment rate peaked. Likewise, the 2002 program was enacted after the recession had ended but before the unemployment rate peaked. The current Emergency Unemployment Compensation (EUC08) program of 2008 was enacted seven months after the most recent recession began.[16]

Table A-1 located in the Appendix briefly summarizes these temporary programs[17] as well as the permanently authorized Extended Benefit (EB) program. The 1982 Federal Supplemental Compensation Benefit (FSB) and 1991 Emergency Unemployment Compensation (EUC) had extremely complicated—and changing—extended benefit triggers. Table A-2 and Table A-3 (also located in the Appendix) provide detailed information on those benefit triggers for those two temporary programs. Table A-4 provides information on the current Emergency Unemployment Compensation (EUC08) program benefits and triggers.

Temporary Extended UC Benefits as Economic Stimulus

In the 110th Congress, congressional and popular debate examined the relative efficacy of expansion of UC benefits and duration compared to other potential economic stimuli. In his January 22, 2008, congressional testimony, the Director of the Congressional Budget Office (CBO) stated that increasing the value or duration of UC benefits may be one of the more effective economic stimulus plans.[18] This is because many of the unemployed are severely cash constrained and would be expected to rapidly spend any increase in benefits that they may receive.[19] Mark Zandi of Moody's *Economy.com* has estimated multiplier effects for several different policy options, including extending unemployment benefits (with multiplier effect of 1.64).[20] The multiplier estimates the increase in total spending in the economy that would result from a dollar spent on a given policy option. Zandi does not explain how these multipliers were estimated, other than to say that they were calculated using his firm's macroeconomic model. Therefore, it is difficult to offer a thorough analysis of the estimates.

Others point out that increasing either the value or length of UC benefits may, however, discourage recipients from searching for work and from accepting less desirable jobs.[21] A rationale for making any extension in unemployment benefits temporary would be to mitigate disincentives to work, as the extension would expire once the economy improves and cyclical unemployment declines.

Assessing the Labor Market: Determining When to Intervene

A variety of measures are typically used to assess the state of the labor market.[22] These measures may include statistics that are absolute measures, such as employment and unemployment levels, as well as relative measures, such as the insured unemployment rate and the total unemployment rate.

A vigorous debate on how to determine when the federal government should intervene by extending unemployment benefits has been active for decades. Generally, this debate has examined the efficacy of using the IUR or TUR as triggers for extending unemployment benefits. The debate also has examined whether the intervention should be at a national or state level. Recently, serious consideration of other measures of the labor market has become increasingly common. In particular, the increase in the number of unemployed from the previous year has emerged in several proposals as a new trigger for a nationwide extension in unemployment benefits.

Improving the UC System as an Automatic Stabilizer

The President's 2010 Budget proposal suggested changes to the UC system through the modification of the EB program in order to make the program more responsive to changing economic conditions.[23] While little information was provided as to the specifics of the legislation, the broad description echoes the recommendations of the Advisory Council on Unemployment Compensation first published in 1994.[24]

Advisory Council on UnemploymentCompensation's 1994 Findings and Recommendations for the Extended Benefit Program

The Advisory Council stated that the changing demographics of the workforce—coupled with state funding problems—had led to a decline in UC recipients. This had, in turn, caused the IUR to be a less reliable indicator of economic conditions at the state level and thus reduced the activation of the state EB program during economic recessions. The Advisory Council also found that the temporary federal extensions of unemployment benefits have been "extremely inefficient" as they were neither well timed nor well targeted.

The Advisory Council generally supported that the EB program use a state TUR of 6.5% as an indicator of economic conditions meriting an active EB program.[25] They also suggested that any indicator not use historical comparisons or thresholds (e.g., 110% of previous year's level) as the Advisory Council labeled them as "not helpful" as they caused the activation of the EB program to occur later and deactivate earlier than what was appropriate.

The Advisory Council did not comment on the cost-sharing provisions of the current EB program.

Finally, the Advisory Council suggested raising the FUTA tax base from $7,000 to $8,500 in order raise the additional funds needed by this suggested change.

Using the Insured Unemployment Rate vs. Total Unemployment Rate

The Federal-State Extended Benefit Program, created by P.L. 91-373, originally assessed the labor market through both insured and "total" unemployment rates and included both national and state level triggers for extended UC benefits. The EB's federal trigger[26] was eliminated by the Omnibus Reconciliation Act of 1980 (P.L. 96-499). That act also required that the IUR measure not include those who had exhausted benefits or who were receiving EB. This effectively made the IUR statistic a less generous measure of unemployment.

Since the adoption of the permanent EB program in 1970, there has been considerable debate concerning the relative merits of the IUR versus the TUR as an EB trigger. The IUR is defined as the 13-week moving average of continuing regular UC claims divided by the average number of individuals in UC-covered employment. This means that the IUR itself is an output of the UC program.

Because the calculation of the IUR is based upon the number of individuals currently receiving UC benefits, each state's IUR depends on various noneconomic factors, including state eligibility rules and administrative practices. Thus, the IUR is not a precise reflection of the health of a state's economy.

In comparison, the TUR is defined as the number of all unemployed individuals actively seeking work divided by the size of the civilian labor force. The TUR represents a larger population than the IUR, because it counts as unemployed all those who are out of work and actively looking for work, on layoff, or waiting to start a new job within 30 days.

National, State, and Sub-State Triggers

A perennial question concerns the appropriate level at which to measure changes in unemployment. Generally this debate has centered on the EB program and whether the EB trigger should be based on national, regional, state or sub-state data. Recently, the debate on the EB trigger has been expanded to ask what measure should be used if a new temporary extension of UC benefits were to be enacted. In particular, should Congress act as it has in the most recent recessions and create a nationwide extension of UC benefits with a nod to higher unemployment states through an additional "high-unemployment" trigger? Or would it be more appropriate and a better use of scarce resources to target only those states with current economic difficulties?

The argument in favor of a national trigger is that the definition of a recession is national in scope, and the federal government's interest in reversing an economic decline is national as well. However, recessions have often been primarily regional in impact. Thus, a national trigger can result in the payment of extended benefits to individuals in states that do not face unusually weak labor markets.

There have also been proposals to create triggers on either a regional or a sub-state level. The logic behind the sub-state or regional triggers is that they might improve the targeting of benefits because state boundaries are often of little relevance to the workings of labor markets. There can be considerable labor market differences between urban and rural areas within a state or among urban areas within a state. Furthermore, some labor markets are located in more than one state. A statewide trigger can deny benefits to areas facing severe labor market problems because other regions of the state are not facing the same conditions. There are a variety of arguments against regional and sub-state triggers. It would be difficult to define appropriate regional or sub-state boundaries, and it is unclear whether these newly defined regions would be any less arbitrary than current state boundaries. In addition, there are significant obstacles to be overcome in the financing and administration of an EB program on the basis of regional or sub-state areas, because the state has always been the operational unit for UC. There is also concern regarding the accuracy and availability of regional or sub-state data and the costs of data improvements that would be needed.[27]

Increases in Unemployment of at Least One Million Unemployed as Compared to the Same Month in the Previous Year

In the 110th Congress, debate moved away from using the IUR or TUR as a trigger for a national program. Serious consideration of other measures of the labor market has become increasingly common. In particular, the increase in the number of unemployed from the previous year has emerged in several proposals for new triggers in a nationwide extension in unemployment benefits.

H.R. 4934, the Emergency Unemployment Compensation Act of 2008, was introduced on January 15, 2008. This bill would have extended UC benefits for up to 26 weeks whenever the number of unemployed persons 16 years of age or older as compared to the same month of the previous year exceeded one million individuals.

Table A-5, located in the Appendix, provides information on the timing of the recessions, changes in unemployment of at least 1 million compared to same month in the previous year, and federal enactment of the temporary extensions of benefits. During this period, the temporary extensions of unemployment benefits take effect between 4 and 14 months after the onset of the recession. The first changes in unemployment compared to the same month in the previous year of at least 1 million occur between 3 and 5 months after the onset of the recession. Therefore, if the use of the 1 million trigger had been applied in the past, the extension of UC benefits would have been triggered between 8 to 12 months earlier than actually occurred.

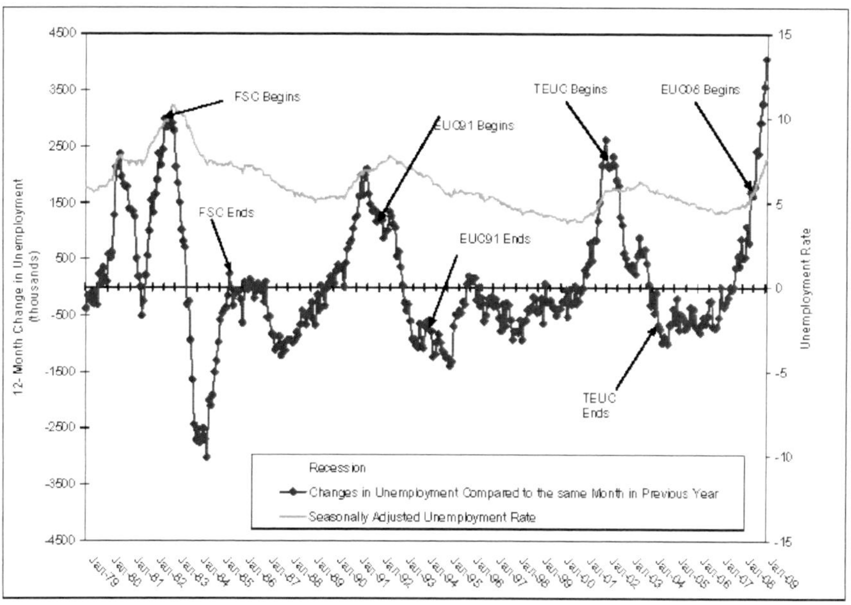

Source: CRS figure. Timing of recessions from National Economic Bureau of Research. Estimated changes in unemployment compared to same month in the previous year from the Current Population Survey data, Bureau of Labor Statistics.

Figure 1. Recessions, Changes in Unemployment Compared to Same Month in Previous Year, Unemployment Rates, and Temporary Federal Benefit Availability, January 1979-January 2009.

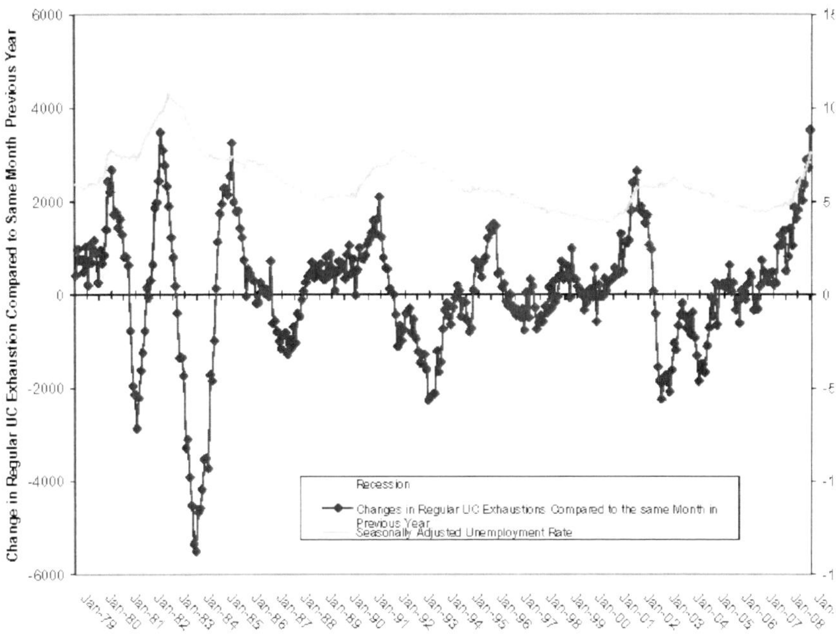

Source: CRS figure. Timing of recessions from National Economic Bureau of Research. Estimated changes in UC benefit exhaustion compared to same month in previous year from the Employment and Training Administration, Department of Labor. Unemployment rate from the Current Population Survey data, Bureau of Labor Statistics, Department of Labor.

Figure 2. Recessions, Changes in Regular UC Benefit Exhaustions as Compared to the Same Month in Previous Year, and Unemployment Rates, January 1979- January 2009.

Figure 1 provides a graphical presentation of the information that was summarized in Table A-4. Figure 1 also includes data on the unemployment rate.

Please note that Figure 1 uses different numerical scales for changes in unemployment levels and for the unemployment rate. Because the correspondence between the two scales was determined by page size rather than by a particular reason, readers should not place any significance in the two lines crossing each other. The scale for the changes in unemployment levels compared to same month in the previous year is located on the left-hand y-axis. The scale for the unemployment rate is located on the right-hand y-axis.

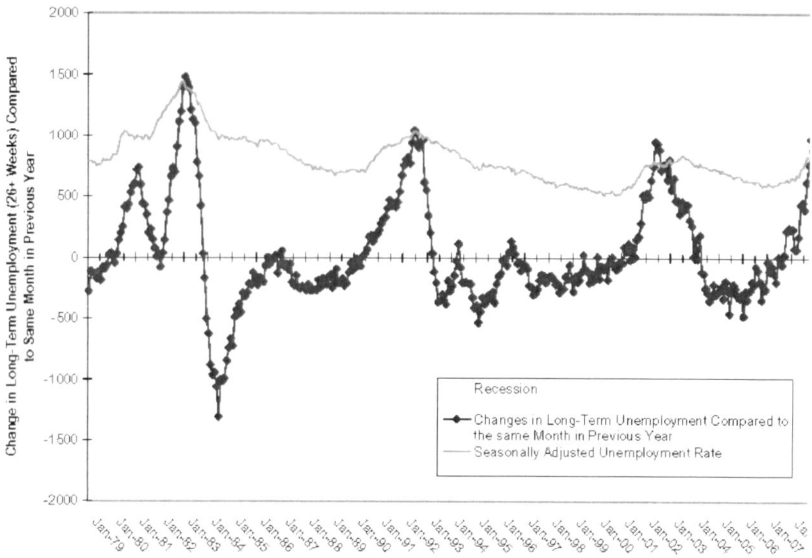

Source: CRS figure. Timing of recessions from National Economic Bureau of Research. Estimated changes in long-term unemployment compared to same month in previous year and unemployment rate from the Current Population Survey data, Bureau of Labor Statistics.

Figure 3. Recessions, Changes in Long-Term Unemployment Compared to the same Month in Previous Year, and Unemployment Rates, January 1979-January 2009.

Other Measures: Changes in Long-Term Unemployment and Changes in UC Benefits Exhaustions

Beyond the IUR, TUR, and changes in the total number of unemployed, several other measures of unemployment are often used in assessing the severity of employment conditions. These measures include the number of unemployed workers who exhaust UC benefits and the number of workers who have been unemployed for more than 26 weeks (the number of long-term unemployed).

Figure 2 shows the change in the number of exhaustion of UC benefits. Figure 3 shows the change in the number of workers who have been unemployed for more than 26 weeks. Generally, both the changes in the numbers of exhaustees and the changes in the number of long-term unemployed peak after the end of a recession.

APPENDIX. RELATED TABLES

Table A- 1. Summary of Extended Unemployment Compensation Programs

Program	Public Law	Dates	Duration of Benefits	Trigger Mechanism	Financing Authority
Temporary Unemployment Compensation (TUC)	P.L. 85-441	Reach back to 6/1957 6/1958 to 6/1959	Lesser of 50% of the regular UC benefit entitlement or 13 weeks.	None.	Interest free loans to state accounts; if a state failed to repay loan by 1/1/63 the FUTA tax in the state was raised to repay the loan.
Temporary Extended Unemployment Compensation (TEUC)	P.L. 87-6	Reach back to 06/1960 04/1961 to 03/1962	Lesser of 50% of the regular UC benefit entitlement or 13 weeks.	None.	FUTA funds.
Federal-State Extended Benefits Act of 1970 (EB)	P.L. 91-373 (Amended several times. See also P.L. 96-499 and P.L. 97-35 below.)	Permanently Authorized	Lesser of 50% of the regular UC benefit entitlement or 13 weeks.	National: IUR: seasonally adjusted rate of at least 4.5% for 3 consecutive months State: IUR: at least 5% and 120% of corresponding	50% state SUTA funds. 50% federal FUTA funds.

Table A- 1. (Continued)

Program	Public Law	Dates	Duration of Benefits	Trigger Mechanism	Financing Authority
				period in prior 2 years; or 6.0%; or TUR: 6.5% and 110% of either of 2 prior years.	
Emergency Unemployment Compensation (Magnuson Act)	P.L. 92-224 and P.L. 92-329	1/1972 to 3/1973	Lesser of 50% of the regular UC benefit entitlement or 13 weeks.	National: IUR: seasonally adjusted rate of at least 4.5% State: IUR: adjusted for exhaustions of at least 4% and 120% of prior 2 years	Federal FUTA funds and general revenue.
Federal Supplemental Benefits (FSB)	P.L. 93-572, P.L. 94-12, P.L. 94-45, and P.L. 95-19	1/1975 to 1/1978	(Varied.) Provided up to 26 weeks of benefits.	National: IUR: seasonally adjusted rate of at least 4.5% State: IUR: at least 5% and 120% prior	Federal FUTA funds for benefits paid before 4/1977; federal general revenue for benefits paid on

Table A- 1. (Continued)

Program	Public Law	Dates	Duration of Benefits	Trigger Mechanism	Financing Authority
				2 years; or 6.0%; or, TUR: 6.5% and 110% of either of 2 prior years.	or after 4/1/1977.
Amendments to Federal-State Extended Benefits Act (EB)	P.L. 96-499 and P.L. 97-35	Permanently Authorized	P.L. 96-499 tightened search and refusal of work requirements. P.L. 97-35 eliminated the national trigger, removed EB recipients from IUR calculations, and required that claimant worked at least 20 weeks recently.	National EB trigger eliminated. State: IUR: at least 5% and 120% prior 13-week period in the previous 2 years; or 6.0%; or, TUR: 6.5% and 110% of either of 2 prior years.	50% state SUTA funds and 50% federal FUTA funds.
Federal Supplemental Compensation (FSC)	P.L. 97-248, P.L. 97-424, P.L. 98-21, P.L. 98-118, P.L. 98-135, and	Reach back to 6/1982 9/1982-6/1985	Varied. See **Table A-2.**	Varied. See **Table A-2.**	Federal FUTA funds and general revenue.

Table A- 1. (Continued)

Program	Public Law	Dates	Duration of Benefits	Trigger Mechanism	Financing Authority
	P.L. 99-15. (P.L. 99-272, some recipients in Pennsylvania.)				
Emergency Unemployment Compensation (EUC)	P.L. 102-164, P.L. 102-182, P.L. 102-244, P.L. 102-318, P.L. 103-6, and P.L. 103-152	Reach back to 2/1991 11/1991-4/1994	Varied. See **Table A-3.** [Note: Supersedes rather than supplements the EB program. Governors had the option of triggering "off" EB benefits.]	Introduced "average" IUR, a 13-week comparison measure. Varied. See **Table A-3.**	Federal FUTA funds for benefits paid before 7/5/1992 and after 10/2/1993; with certain exceptions, federal general revenue for bene-fits paid on or after 7/5/1992 but before 10/3/1993.
Temporary Extended Unemployment Compensation (TEUC, TEUC-X)	P.L. 107-147, P.L. 108-1, and P.L. 108-26	Reach back to 3/2001 3/2002-3/2004	TEUC: Up to 13 weeks. High unemployment states (TEUC-X); up to an additional 13 weeks.	TEUC was availa-ble nationally. TEUC-X was determined by state level: if the EB program was triggered on; or if the EB program	Federal FUTA funds.

Table A- 1. (Continued)

Program	Public Law	Dates	Duration of Benefits	Trigger Mechanism	Financing Authority
				would have been triggered on if section 203(d) of the Federal-State Unemployment Compensation Act of 1970 were amended to read IUR: at least 4% and 120% of the prior 2 years.	
Emergency Unemployment Compensation of 2008 (EUC08)	P.L. 110-252, P.L. 110-449, and P.L. 111-5	Reach back to 5/2007 7/6/2008-12/31/2009	Varied. See **Table A-4**.	EUC08 is nationally available High Unemployment Tier II EUC08 is determined at the state level: if the state TUR is at least 6% or if the state IUR is at least 4%.	Federal FUTA funds. Benefits after February 17, 2009, were paid by general revenue.

Source: CRS.

Table A-2. Details: Federal Supplemental Compensation (FSC) Benefits

Public Law	Benefit Tiers	Dates in Effect (first claim date)
Tax Equity and Fiscal Responsibility Act (P.L. 97-248), signed 9/2/1982.	10 weeks: EB activated in state after 6/1/1982 8 weeks: EB inactive in state; IUR at least 3.5% 6 weeks: all other states.	9/12/1982-1/8/1983.
Surface Transportation Act of 1982 (P.L. 97-424), signed 1/6/1983.	16 weeks: IUR of 6% or higher 14 weeks: EB activated on or after 6/1/1983 but IUR below 6% 12 weeks: IUR at least 4.5% 10 weeks: IUR at least 3.5% but less than 4.5% 8 weeks: all other states	1/9/1983-3/31/1983.
Social Security Amendments of 1983 (P.L. 98-21), signed 4/20/1983.	*First FSC payments on 4/1/1983 orlater:* 14 weeks: IUR of 6% or higher 12 weeks: IUR of at least 5% but less than 6% 10 weeks: IUR of at least 4% but less than 5% 8 weeks: All other states Additional entitlements for FSC recipients before 4/1/1983 10 weeks: IUR at least 6% 8 weeks: IUR at least 4% but less than 6% 6 weeks: all other states	4/1/1983-10/18/1983.
Federal Supplemental Compensation Amendments of 1983 (P.L. 98-135), signed 10/24/1983.	*FSC first payments on 10/19/1983 or later:* 14 weeks: IUR of 6% or higher 12 weeks: IUR of at least 5% but less than 6% 10 weeks: IUR of at least 4% but less than 5% 8 weeks: all other states	10/19/1983-3/31/1985. (No benefits past 6/1985).

Table A-2. (Continued)

Public Law	Benefit Tiers	Dates in Effect (first claim date)
	Additional entitlements for FSC recipients after 3/31/1983 but before 10/19/1983 5 weeks: if all remaining benefits are for weeks before 10/19/1983 4 weeks: IUR of at least 5% 2 weeks: all other states	

Source: CRS.

Table A-3. Details: Emergency Unemployment Compensation (EUC) Benefits of 1991

Public Law	Benefit Tiers	Dates in Effect (first claim date)
Emergency Unemployment Compensation Act (P.L. 102-164), signed 11/15/1991.	20 weeks: States with TUR of 9.5% or higher or IUR of 5% or higher. 13 weeks: States with IUR of 4% or higher or IUR of 2.5% or higher and UC exhaustion rate of 29% or higher. 6 weeks: All other states.	Superseded by P.L. 102-182.
Termination of Application of Title IV of the Trade Act of 1974 to Czechoslovakia and Hungary (P.L. 102-182), signed 12/4/1991; and Emergency Unemployment Benefits Extension (P.L. 102-244), signed 2/7/1992.	*Claims filed before 6/14/1992* 33 weeks: States with TUR of 9% or higher or IUR of 5% or higher. 26 weeks: All other states. *Claims filed on or after 6/14/1992* 20 weeks: States with TUR of 9% or higher or IUR of 5% or higher. 13 weeks: All other states. [Note: P.L. 102-182 authorized benefit periods of 20 and 13 weeks; P.L. 102-244 authorized an additional 13 weeks for each tier.]	11/17/1991-7/3/1992.

Table A-3. (Continued)

Public Law	Benefit Tiers	Dates in Effect (first claim date)
Unemployment Compensation Amendments of 1992 (P.L. 102-318), signed 7/3/1992.	26 weeks: States with TUR of 9% or higher or IUR of 5% or higher 20 weeks: All other states. [Note: If national TUR fell below 7.0% benefits were to be phased down. This condition was not met.]	6/14/1992-3/6/1993.
Emergency Unemployment Compensation Amendments of 1993 (P.L. 103-6), signed 3/4/1993.	*Claims filed before 9/12/1993* 26 weeks: states with TUR of 9% or higher or IUR of 5% or higher 20 weeks: all other states Claims filed on or after 9/12/1993 (triggered by national TUR falling below 7% for 2 consecutive months) 15 weeks: States with TUR of 9% or higher or IUR of 5% or higher. 10 weeks: All other states.	3/7/1993-10/2/1993.
Unemployment Compensation Amendments of 1993 (P.L. 103-152), signed 11/25/1993	13 weeks: States with TUR of 9% or higher or IUR of 5% or higher. 7 weeks: All other states. [Note: This law also made permanent changes to the EB program to make its benefits more widely available after the expiration of EUC.]	10/3/1993-2/5/1994 (No benefits past 4/30/1994)

Source: CRS.

Table A-4. Details: Emergency Unemployment Compensation (EUC08) Benefits of 2008

Public Law	Benefit Tiers	Dates in Effect (first claim date)
Supplemental Appropriations Act of 2008, Title IV Emergency Unemployment Compensation (P.L. 110-252), signed June 30, 2008	13 weeks: all states	7/6/2008-3/29/2009 (No benefits past 7/4/2009)

Table A-4. (Continued)

Public Law	Benefit Tiers	Dates in Effect (first claim date)
Unemployment Compensation Extension Act of 2008, (P.L. 110-449), signed November 21, 2008.	33 weeks: states with TUR of 6% or higher or IUR of 4% or higher 20 weeks: all other states	11/23/2008-3/29/2009 (No benefits past 8/29/2009)
American Recovery and Reinvestment Act of 2009, P.L. 111-5, signed February 17, 2009.	33 weeks: states with TUR of 6% or higher or IUR of 4% or higher 20 weeks: all other states	2/17/2009-12/26/2009 (No benefits past 6/6/2010)
	[Note this included several other interventions that augmented UC benefits. The Federal Additional Compensation benefit of $25/week for those receiving UC, EUC08, EB, DUA, or TRA. At state option, EB benefit year could be calculated based upon exhausting EUC08 benefits. First $2400 of unemployment benefits were excluded from income tax in 2009.]	

Source: CRS.

Table A-5. Timing of Recessions, Changes in Unemployment of at Least One Million Unemployed Compared to Same Month in Previous Year, and Extended Unemployment Benefits, 1990-2008

	1980 Recession		1981-1982 Recession		1990-1991 Recession		2001 Recession		2007 Recession	
	Temporary Federal Extension	Months after Recession Begins	P.L. 97-248, FSC Benefits	Months after Recession Begins	P.L. 102-164, EUC Benefits	Months after Recession Begins	P.L. 107-147, TEUC Benefits	Months after Recession Begins	P.L. 110-252, EUC08 Benefits	Months after Recession Begins
Date began	January 1980	—	July 1981	—	July 1990	—	March 2001	—	December 2007	—
First change in unemployment of at least 1 million compared to same month in previous year	April 1980	3 months	November 1981	4 months	November 1990	4 months	August 2001	5 months	March 2008	3 months
Congress first enacts extension	Nonea	NA	August 1982	13 months	August 1991	13 months	February 2002	11 months	June 2008	6 months
Program becomes active	None	NA	September 1982	14 months	November 1991[b,c]	16 months	March 2002	12 months	July 2008	7 months
End recession	July 1980	6 months	November 1982	16 months	March 1991	8 months	November 2001	8 months	To be determined (TBD)	—
Last change of at least 1 million unemployed	March 1981	14 months	April 1983	21 months	September 1992	17 months	September 2002	20 months	TBD	—

Table A-5. (Continued)

	1980 Recession		1981-1982 Recession		1990-1991 Recession		2001 Recession		2007 Recession	
	Temporary Federal Extension	Months after Recession Begins	P.L. 97-248, FSC Benefits	Months after Recession Begins	P.L. 102-164, EUC Benefits	Months after Recession Begins	P.L. 107-147, TEUC Benefits	Months after Recession Begins	P.L. 110-252, EUC08 Benefits	Months after Recession Begins
Last benefits claimed	NA	NA	June 1985	47 months	April 1994	44 months	April 2004	37 months	Scheduled: April 2010	Scheduled: 28 months

Source: CRS. Timing of recessions from National Economic Bureau of Research http://www.nber.org/cycles.html. Estimated increases of 1 million unemployed use data from the Current Population Survey, Bureau of Labor Statistics; http://www.bls.gov/data/home.htm.

a. The individual eligibility for the federal-state EB program was tightened by P.L. 96-499. The federal EB trigger was eliminated and the calculation of IUR was altered to be less generous by P.L. 97-35.

b. H.R. 3201 was passed on 8/2/1991; the President signed the bill (P.L. 102-107) but did not declare an emergency; thus, no benefits were available. Congress sent S. 1722 to the President who vetoed it on 10/1/1991. For a statement on the reasons for the veto, see http://www.presidency

c. Although P.L. 102-164 was signed into law on November 15, 1991, it was immediately superseded by 2 other laws: P.L. 102-182, signed 12/4/1991, and P.L. 102-244, signed 2/7/1992. P.L. 102-182 authorized benefit periods of 20 and 13 weeks depending on state economic conditions; P.L. 1 02-244 authorized an additional 13 weeks for each tier.

End Notes

[1] For more information on UC, CRS Report RL33362, *Unemployment Insurance: Available Unemployment Benefits and Legislative Activity*, by Alison M. Shelton and Julie M. Whittaker. For information on the most recent temporary federal unemployment benefit extension, see CRS Report RS22915, *Temporary Extension of Unemployment Benefits: Emergency Unemployment Compensation (EUC08)*, by Julie M. Whittaker and Alison M. Shelton.

[2] The percent of UC beneficiaries as compared to all unemployed workers is commonly referred to as the "recipiency rate." The exhaustion rate measures the proportion of all UC benefit recipients who exhaust their UC eligibility and do not find a job within that period.

[3] For a detailed survey of this disincentive effect, see Burtless, Gary. "Unemployment Insurance and Labor Supply: A Survey." In *Unemployment Insurance*, W. Lee Hansen and James Byers, eds. Madison: University of Wisconsin Press.

[4]Burtless, Gary. "Unemployment Insurance and Labor Supply: A Survey." In *Unemployment Insurance*, W. Lee Hansen and James Byers, eds. Madison: University of Wisconsin Press.

[5] See CRS Report RL321 11, *Unemployment Compensation (UC)/ Unemployment Insurance (UI): Trends and Contributing Factors in UC Benefit Exhaustion*, by Julie M. Whittaker.

[6] Corson, Walter and Mark Dynarski. *A Study of Unemployment Insurance Recipients and Exhaustees: Findings from a National Survey*. Unemployment Insurance Occasional Paper 90-3. U.S. Department of Labor Employment and Training Administration, 1990.

[7] These services may include training on job search, job counseling, and funding for educational and skill-enhancing courses.

[8] For details on these trends, see CRS Report RL32757, *Unemployment and Older Workers*, by Julie M. Whittaker.

[9] For a detailed explanation on the determination of recessions, see CRS Report RS22793, *What is a Recession, Who Decides When It Starts, and When Do They Decide?*, by Brian W. Cashell.

[10] The NBER explicitly states that it considers real GDP to be the single measure that comes closest to capturing what it means by "aggregate economic activity." Therefore, it places considerable weight on real GDP and other output measures. Thus, the NBER takes into account employment but not unemployment or unemployment rates when determining recessionary periods. The NBER's approach is summarized at *http://www.nber.org/cycles*

[11] See, for example, President Franklin Roosevelt's remarks at the signing of the Social Security Act: http://www.ssa.gov/history/fdrstmts.html#signing.

[12] The IUR is the ratio of persons receiving UC benefits to the number of persons covered by UC. The IUR is substantially different than the TUR because it excludes several important groups: self-employed workers, unpaid family workers, workers in certain not-for-profit organizations, and several other, primarily seasonal, categories of workers. In addition to those unemployed workers whose last jobs were in the excluded employment, the insured unemployed rate excludes the following: those who have exhausted their UC benefits; new entrants or reentrants to the labor force; disqualified workers whose unemployment is considered to have resulted from their own actions rather than from economic conditions; and, eligible unemployed persons who do not file for benefits.

[13] The TUR is essentially a weekly version of the unemployment rate published by the Bureau of Labor Statistics: that is, the ratio of the total number of unemployed persons divided by the total number of employed and unemployed persons.

[14] According to the *2008 Comparison of State Unemployment Insurance Laws* the following states require at least one of the "20 weeks" requirements for regular UC benefits: Alabama, Colorado, Connecticut, Florida, Georgia, Kentucky, Louisiana, Michigan, Mississippi,

Missouri, New York, North Dakota, Ohio, South Carolina, South Dakota, Tennessee, and Utah.

[15] For additonal information, see CRS Report R40368, *Unemployment Insurance Provisions in the American Recovery and Reinvestment Act of 2009*, by Alison M. Shelton, Kathleen Romig, and Julie M. Whittaker.

[16] For a detailed description of the EUC08 program, see CRS Report RS22915, *Temporary Extension of Unemployment Benefits: Emergency Unemployment Compensation (EUC08)*, by Julie M. Whittaker and Alison M. Shelton.

[17] The summary does not include P.L. 108-11, which created the special "TEUC-A" program. That temporary program was in response to the unemployment of airline workers resulting from the September 11, 2001, terrorist attacks, subsequent security measures, and the Iraq war. Signed into law on April 16, 2003, the program provided up to 39 weeks of extended benefits to individuals whose regular UC was based on qualifying employment with a certified air carrier, at a facility in an airport, or with a producer or supplier of products or services for an air carrier. The program had two tiers of benefits, known as TEUC-A and TEUC-AX and were authorized through the week ending before December 29, 2003.

[18] See CBO Testimony of Peter Orszag on Options for Responding to Short-Term Economic Weakness before the Committee on Finance United States Senate on January 22, 2008; http://www.cbo.gov/ftpdocs/89xx/doc8932/01-22- TestimonyEconStimulus.pdf.

[19] For another paper that takes this position, see the following: Elmendorf, Douglas W. and Jason Furman, *If, When, How: A Primer on Fiscal Stimulus,* January 2008; available at http://www.brookings.edu/papers/2008/*011 0*_fiscal_stimulus_elmendorf_furman.aspx.

[20] Mark Zandi, "Washington Throws the Economy a Rope," Dismal Scientist, Moody's *Economy.com*, January 22, 2008.

[21] For example, Shrek, James and Patrick Tyrell, *Unemployment Insurance Does Not Stimulate the Economy*, Webmemo #1777, January 2008; *http://www.heritage.org/Research /Economy/wm1777.cfm#_ftn1.* See also Martin Feldstein's testimony before the Committee on Finance United States on January 24, 2008, in which he stated that "[w]hile raising unemployment benefits or extending the duration of benefits beyond 26 weeks would help some individuals ... it would also create undesirable incentives for individuals to delay returning to work. That would lower earnings and total spending." Available at http://www.senate.gov/~finance/hearings/testimony/2008test/ 012408mftest.pdf.

[22] For a detailed explanation of the more common employment measures, see CRS Report RL32642, *Employment Statistics: Differences and Similarities in Job-based and Person-based Employment and Unemployment Estimates*, by Julie M. Whittaker.

[23] See the http://www.whitehouse.gov/omb/assets

[24] Advisory Council on Unemployment Compensation, "1994 Findings and Recommendations: Extended Benefits," in *Collected Findings and Recommendations: 1994-1996. Reprinted from Annual Reports of the Advisory Council on Unemployment Compensation to the President and Congress.* (Washington, DC 1996).

[25] The Advisory Council also suggested that a modified IUR that also included those who had exhausted UC benefit in the IUR calculation would be superior to the current IUR calculation.

[26] The federal trigger was an IUR of at least 4.5% for 3 consecutive months.

[27] The Advisory Council on Unemployment Compensation advised against the use of substate or regional data in determining the availability of extended benefits. Advisory Council on Unemployment Compensation, *Collected Findings and Recommendations: 1994-1996*, 1996. p. 5.

In: Recession, Depression, and Unemployment ISBN: 978-1-61761-508-5
Editors: Daniel A. García

Chapter 5

THE LABOR MARKET DURING THE GREAT DEPRESSION AND THE CURRENT RECESSION

Linda Levine

SUMMARY

A good deal of commentary has addressed similarities between the recession that began in December 2007 and the Great Depression. Comparisons between the two have extended beyond conditions in financial markets to conditions in the labor market. The analogy appears to be fueled by projections that the unemployment rate could reach double digits in the coming months.

Little if any comparative labor market research has been undertaken, however. To address the situation, this chapter analyzes the experiences of workers during the 1930s, which encompassed the almost five years of the Great Depression. Because it was a period very distant and different from today, the report devotes considerable time to examining the employment and unemployment measures then available. The report ends by comparing the labor market conditions of the 1930s with those encountered by workers thus far during the nation's eleventh recession of the post-World War II period.

A labor market analysis of the Great Depression finds that many workers were unemployed for much longer than one year. Of those fortunate to have jobs, many experienced cutbacks in hours (i.e., involuntary part-time employment). Men typically were more adversely affected than women. This was especially true for older and black men at a time when age- and race-based job discrimination were not unlawful and when occupational shifts in labor demand were operating against them. Higher-skilled workers fared better than lower-skilled workers. Those who toiled on farms and in factories were displaced in very large numbers. States whose economies were dependent on agriculture and manufacturing reported high unemployment rates.

There are several similarities not only between the Great Depression and the recession that began in December 2007, but also between the Great Depression and other recent recessions. They include the greater impact of economic downturns on male blue-collar workers in the goods-producing sector (e.g., construction and manufacturing), lower-skilled workers, and older workers.

But, there remain substantial differences between the Great Depression and the current recession:

- In 1933, at the depth of the Depression, one in four workers was unemployed. In contrast, the unemployment rate had risen to 9.4% by May 2009. The number of jobs on nonfarm payrolls fell 24.3% between 1929 and 1933. Thus far during the current recession, firms have cut nonfarm employment by 4.3%. The first 17 months of the ongoing recession compare favorably with the first two years of the Depression as well.
- In addition to the greater magnitude of unemployment and job loss during the early 1930s as compared with today, the implications of being unemployed have changed much in the intervening years. One reason for the altered situation facing today's unemployed is the increased prevalence of families in which both spouses work. Another is the deeper drop in earnings and hours worked that occurred during the Depression. And, the social safety net that is now available to displaced workers and their families did not exist before the onset of the Great Depression.

References often have been made to similarities between the Great Depression and the recession that began in December 2007. Both were preceded by long periods of economic Rexpansion during which consumers financed many of their purchases by taking on considerable debt. The substantial losses in savings that resulted from the bank failures of the 1930s made it all the more difficult for individual and commercial depositors to continue spending and investing to the degree they had previously. Today, credit also has become difficult for individuals and businesses to obtain—not because of bank failures, given the availability of federal deposit insurance, but rather because risky investments have led to deteriorated balance sheets at some banks and other financial institutions that have impaired their ability to extend credit.[1]

Comparisons between the Great Depression and the eleventh recession of the post-World War II period have extended beyond conditions in the financial market to conditions in the labor market. Speculation that the unemployment rate could reach double digits in the coming months appears to have fueled the analogy. Little if any comparative research has been undertaken, however.

This chapter analyzes the labor market experiences of workers during the 1930s, which encompassed the almost five years of the Great Depression. Because it was a period very distant and different from today, considerable time is devoted to examining the employment and unemployment measures available at that time. The report ends by comparing the labor market conditions of the 1930s with those encountered by workers thus far during the recession that began in December 2007.

THE LABOR MARKETDURING THE GREAT DEPRESSION

Analysis of labor market conditions during the Great Depression is complicated by the fact that "throughout the worst years of the Depression, no one knew how many unemployed persons there were, much less their characteristics," because not until March 1940 did the federal government initiate a monthly survey of the labor force defined much as it is today.[2] In 1937, the 75th Congress passed Pub. Law No. 409, which required the President to conduct a census of unemployment.[3] At least one of the 14-question Unemployment Report Cards was delivered by postal carriers to each dwelling in the United States and additional cards were made available at local post offices to the "employable unemployed." But, the 1940 census of the population was the first statistical undertaking to include questions on the labor force defined as persons who are employed or without jobs but actively seeking work within a prescribed period of time. Before then, the 1930 census of the population, the 1937 census of unemployment, and the occasional survey conducted in various states and cities utilized a very different concept—the "gainful worker"—that is, individuals who had at some time worked in an occupation in which they earned money or the equivalent, or in which they assisted in the production of marketable goods. Different occupational classification systems also were utilized in the 1930 and 1940 population censuses. For these reasons, this section of the report relies greatly on the U.S. Census Bureau's adjustment of selected data from the 1930 census to make it as consistent as possible with the 1940 census. [4] The **Appendix** discusses the evolution of labor force data over time. It is intended to supplement information in the detailed table notes in the body of the report about the specific Depression-era data presented in the tables.

Employment

What commonly is referred to as the Great Depression comprised two downturns in the business cycle. The first recession began in August 1929, and lasted 43 months until March 1933. A sluggish comeback of the economy occurred during the next four years, before the business cycle peaked in May 1937. The subsequent 13-month decline in the economy's performance ended in June 1938, but employment did not fully recover until the United States entered World War II.

Demographic and OccupationalCharacteristics

The percentage of the working-age population employed fell substantially between 1930 and 1940, as shown in **Table 1**. Virtually all of the decrease occurred among men, with the proportion of the male population with jobs dropping 10 percentage points to 67.5%.

Men continued to dominate the ranks of the employed during the 1930s despite the Great Depression's very different impact by gender. The number of men employed fell by 898,000 over the decade, while the number of women employed rose by almost 1.3 million. Women's share of employed persons consequently grew to one-fourth by 1940.

Employers' hiring decisions partly account for the differential employment effect of the Great Depression by age group. The substantial decrease in employment among teenagers (14- to 19-year-olds) likely was associated with the last-hired/first-fired approach that employers traditionally observe. Additionally, with passage of the Fair Labor Standards Act (FLSA) in 1938, the age limit for employment in manufacturing industries was raised to 16 years, which effectively reduced the number of job opportunities for young persons. This, in turn, might have prompted some teenagers to refrain from entering the workforce and instead, remain voluntarily in school after reaching age 14. School attendance requirements were increased over the decade in some geographic areas as well.[5]

The order in which employers usually conduct layoffs varies inversely with seniority, which would be expected to benefit older workers. But, length of service is of no help to older workers if entire plants are closed and all employees are let go. Once laid off, older workers found it particularly difficult to find new jobs. Because age discrimination was not unlawful at the time, employers could refuse with impunity to hire older workers if they generalized that younger workers were more adaptable and possessed more up-to-date skills, for example. "During the 1930s many firms adopted a policy of not hiring anyone over some stated maximum age, the limit being placed sometimes as low as 45 years or even lower."[6]

The varying impact of technological developments by occupation also helps to explain the differing pattern of job loss across gender and age groups. Increased mechanization and the advent of the assembly line permitted substitution of semiskilled workers for skilled workers, which operated to the advantage of women and younger men compared to older men.[7] As shown in Table 2, the proportion of workers in skilled occupations fell from 12.9% to 11.7% between 1930 and 1940, with the entire decrease occurring among men. Older men in particular were displaced by mechanization because skilled workers more often were age 45 and older.[8] In contrast, few women worked in skilled occupations (0.8% in 1930) while many more worked in the growing semiskilled occupations (23.7% in 1930).

In part because mechanization also could substitute for physical strength, the demand for unskilled workers fell as well. This, too, adversely affected men to a greater extent than women because men more often were unskilled farm and nonfarm (construction and factory) laborers whose jobs could be replaced by machinery. (See Table 2.) Black men in particular were susceptible to the shift in demand away from unskilled jobs because the occupations of farm and nonfarm laborers accounted for 43% of employed black men compared to 17% of employed white men.[9] In contrast, unskilled women primarily were servants whose jobs could not as readily be supplanted by machinery.

Women also fared better than men during the Depression due to the increased demand for workers in white-collar occupations (e.g., professional and clerical workers). Growth in white-collar occupations was especially pronounced among clerical and related workers, which, as seen in **Table 2**, was the single largest employment category for women. In contrast, men's concentration in the farm operator category meant that they suffered most directly the consequences of the shift from an agrarian to an industrial economy. Black men were especially vulnerable: farm owners and tenants accounted for 21% of black men's employment in 1940 compared to 14% of white men's employment.[10]

Table 1. Employment by Gender and Age, 1930 and 1940 (Numbers in Thousands)

Gender and Age	Number Employed		Employment as a Percent of Population	
	1930	1940	1930	1940
Total	44,953	45,338	50.5%	44.8%
Men	34,997	34,099	77.6	67.5
14-19 years	2,575	1,752	36.9	23.7
20-24 years	4,409	3,961	82.5	69.6
25-44 years	16,652	16,456	91.2	83.6
45-64 years	9,645	10,256	86.2	76.7
65 years and over	1,716	1,674	51.5	38.0
Women	9,956	11,239	22.6	22.2
14-19 years	1,445	961	20.7	13.1
20-24 years	2,222	2,263	40.1	38.4
25-44 years	4,264	5,515	23.8	27.6
45-64 years	1,786	2,243	17.4	17.6
65 years and over	239	257	7.2	5.6

Source: U.S. Bureau of the Census, *Sixteenth Census of the United States: 1940, Population: Estimates of Labor Force, Employment and Unemployment in the United States, 1940 and 1930*, Washington, DC, 1944.

Notes: In the 1930 census, individuals were asked to report whether they were at work yesterday (i.e., the day before the enumerator called) in which case they were counted as employed. If they responded otherwise, they were asked into which of seven classifications of unemployment they fell. Based on newly introduced definitions of employment and unemployment, the 1940 census would have considered some individuals in the seven classifications to be employed. The Census Bureau adjusted estimates in the 1930 and 1940 decennial censuses for this and other differences to make the data as consistent as possible. For further explanation of the adjusted data that appear in the table see the **Appendix**.

Table 2. Occupational Distribution of Gainful Workers in 1930 and of the Experienced Labor Force in 1940, by Gender (number of persons age 14 and older in thousands)

Occupation and Gender	Number of Gainful Workers[a]	Number in the Experienced Labor Force[b]	Percent Distribution	
	1930	1940	1930	1940
Total	*48,595*	*52,020*	*100.0%*	*100.0%*
Professionals	2,946	3,382	6.1	6.5
Proprietors, managers, and officials	9,665	9,234	19.9	17.8
Farmers (owners and tenants)	6,012	5,275	12.4	10.0
Clerical, sales, and related workers	7,936	8,924	16.3	17.2
Skilled workers and supervisors	6,283	6,105	12.9	11.7
Semiskilled workers	7,973	10,918	16.4	21.0
Unskilled workers	13,792	13,457	28.4	25.9
Nonfarm laborers	6,273	5,566	12.9	10.7
Farm laborers	4,187	3,708	8.6	7.1
Servants	3,332	4,182	6.9	8.0
Men	*37,916*	*39,446*	*100.0%*	*100.0%*
Professionals	1,498	1,847	4.0	4.7
Proprietors, managers, and officials	9,160	8,702	24.2	22.1
Farmers (owners and tenants)	5,749	5,121	15.2	13.0
Clerical, sales, and related workers	4,865	5,269	12.8	13.4
Skilled workers and supervisors	6,202	6,001	16.4	15.1
Semiskilled workers	5,444	7,336	14.4	18.6
Unskilled workers	10,747	10,292	28.3	26.1
Nonfarm laborers	6,116	5,437	16.1	13.8
Farm laborers	3,607	3,362	9.5	8.5
Servants	1,024	1,492	2.7	3.8
Women	*10,679*	*12,574*	*100.0%*	*100.0%*
Professionals	1,448	1,535	13.6	12.2
Proprietors, managers, and officials	506	532	4.7	4.2
Farmers (owners and tenants)	263	154	2.5	1.2
Clerical, sales, and related workers	3,072	3,655	28.8	29.1

Table 2. (Continued)

Occupation and Gender	Number of Gainful Workers[a]	Number in the Experienced Labor Force[b]	Percent Distribution	
	1930	1940	1930	1940
Skilled workers and supervisors	81	104	0.8	0.8
Semiskilled workers	2,528	3,582	23.7	28.5
Unskilled workers	3,045	3,165	28.5	25.2
Nonfarm laborers	156	130	1.5	1.0
Farm laborers	580	346	5.4	2.7
Servants	2,308	2,690	21.6	21.4

Source: U.S. Bureau of the Census, *Sixteenth Census of the United States: 1940, Population: Comparative Occupation Statistics for the United States*, 1870 to 1940, Washington, D.C., 1943.

a. Gainful workers are employed and unemployed persons who reported having a gainful occupation, i.e., an occupation in which they earned money or a money equivalent, or in which they assisted in the production of marketable goods, regardless of their activity at the time the 1930 census was conducted. Although in 1930 and earlier censuses gainful workers between 10 and 13 years old were counted, the Census Bureau excluded them from the data presented in the above table because only persons age 14 and older were included as members of the labor force in the 1940 census. The Bureau made other adjustments to the 1930 count of gainful workers to make the data comparable with the labor force concept introduced in the 1940 census. See the Appendix for additional information.

b. The size of the experienced labor force is based on a complete count of persons age 14 and older employed for pay or profit (or at unpaid family work) by occupation at the time the 1940 decennial census was taken and a 5% cross-section sample count of the usual occupations of experienced workers seeking jobs and of persons on public emergency work at the time the 1940 census was taken.

IndustryCharacteristics

No industry except government was immune from the Great Depression. According to the U.S. Bureau of Labor Statistics' annual count of jobs on the payrolls of nonfarm employers, employment dropped by 7.6 million or 24.3% between 1929 and 1933.[11] Almost three out of every five jobs lost were from the goods-producing sector, where employment fell by one-third from 13.3 million to less than 9 million. (See Table 3.) Within the goods-producing sector, construction and manufacturing workers were the hardest hit: by 1933, there were 45.5% fewer construction jobs and 30.9% fewer manufacturing jobs than in 1929. In absolute terms, manufacturing accounted for over three-fourths of all job losses in the sector. Manufacturers of durable goods bore much of the decrease, with motor vehicle and equipment firms providing 45.5% fewer factory jobs in 1933 than in 1929 for example.[12]

During the 1937-1938 downturn, job losses were even more concentrated in the goods-producing sector. Over three-fourths of the almost 2 million jobs lost in that year were in mining, construction and manufacturing industries. Manufacturing accounted for almost nine out of ten (1.4 out of 1.5 million) job losses in the sector. The milder second downturn produced relatively fewer job cutbacks than the first downturn at manufacturers (12.5%) and construction firms (5.1%).

Table 3. Employees on Nonfarm Payrolls by Major Industry Group in Peak and Trough Years of the Great Depression (numbers in thousands)

Industry	1929	1933	1937	1938
All nonfarm industries	31,324	23,699	31,011	29,194
Goods- Producing sector	13,301	8,965	12,936	11,401
Mining	1,087	744	1,015	891
Construction	1,512	824	1,127	1,070
Manufacturing	10,702	7,397	10,794	9,440
Service- providing sector	18,023	14,734	18,075	17,793
Transportation and public utilities	3,916	2,672	3,134	2,863
Wholesale and retail trade	6,123	4,755	6,265	6,179
Finance, insurance, and real estate	n.a.	n.a.	n.a.	1,447
Services	n.a.	n.a.	n.a.	3,502
Government (excludes public Emergency workers)	3,065	3,166	3,756	3,883

Source: U.S. Bureau of Labor Statistics, *Employment, Hours, and Earnings, United States, 1909-90*, Bulletin 2370, vol. I and II, Washington, D.C., 1991.

Notes: The Current Employment Statistics (CES) program queries nonfarm employers about the number of jobs on their payrolls, and therefore, excludes self-employed persons and unpaid family workers who are counted in censuses and surveys of the population. However, employer surveys are considered a more accurate count of employment than can be gleaned from individuals through population censuses and surveys. n.a.=not available.

Companies in the service-producing sector also felt the Depression's influence as laid off workers became unable to afford their former level of purchases at such establishments as grocers and clothing stores. Employment in the service-producing sector declined by 3.3 million jobs or 18.2% during the 1929-1933 downturn. Job losses in the sector numbered 282,000 or 1.6% during the second downturn of the decade.

Agricultural employment fell as well during the 1930s. Droughts and dust storms led farm families to migrate from such states as Oklahoma and Arkansas, and the introduction of technological innovations (e.g., tractors, combines, mechanical cotton and corn pickers) displaced sharecropper families.[13] The number of persons working in agriculture was estimated to have been about 10.5 million in 1929.[14] Farm employment decreased steadily to about 10.0 million by 1933. It remained largely unchanged through 1937, after which the decline in farm employment resumed.

Part-time Employment

Of the 2.5 million workers on the payrolls of the 6,551 firms that responded to a federal government questionnaire sent to 25,000 firms in March 1932, 56% were employed part-time. Part-timers were even more prevalent in manufacturing industries in which they represented 63% of all workers at the companies that responded. The high incidence of part-time employment was involuntary; that is, people worked fewer hours than they would have preferred due to the low operating rates at the surveyed firms. Only 26% of the responding firms were operating on full-time schedules and only 28% were open five or more days a week. [15]

Part-time employment also was a deliberate strategy pursued under both the Hoover and Roosevelt Administrations. "Work-sharing" was intended to spread across employees the scarcer work hours that resulted from greatly reduced demand for goods and services. But,

> [w]here President Hoover had tried to prevent the loss of some jobs by persuading industry leaders to cut hours, President Roosevelt tried, with some success, to reemploy many of those who had lost jobs by cutting hours still further and establishing minimum wages.[16]

Before the National Industrial Recovery Act was declared unconstitutional in 1935, "business adopted voluntary codes, including minimum wages and maximum hours. These foreshadowed the Fair Labor Standards Act of 1938," which "contained a work sharing measure in the form of an overtime penalty for weekly hours more than 40."[17]

Unemployment

The unemployment rate rose from 3.2% in 1929 to 24.9% in 1933 during the Great Depression's more severe first downturn. While almost 1.6 million persons were unemployed in 1929, more than 12.8 million individuals lacked jobs in 1933. The unemployment rate declined during the brief recovery and measured 14.3% in 1937, when the second downturn began. Although the Great Depression came to an end in June 1938, the unemployment rate averaged 19.0% for the year. The number of unemployed persons jumped by almost 3 million (from 7.7 million to 10.4 million) between 1937 and 1938.[18]

DemographicCharacteristics

Gender

In relative terms, women experienced a greater increase in unemployment than men (304% and 208%, respectively) between 1930 and 1940. (See Table 4.) Contributing to the elevated joblessness of women was their entering the labor force at an accelerated pace during such poor economic times, which they did in part to compensate for the unemployment of their spouses.[19] Although the percentage of women unemployed rose during the 1930s, their unemployment rate remained below that of men at 13.6% and 15.4%, respectively, in 1940. The Census Bureau suggested that this might be explained by women being more likely to leave the labor force upon losing their jobs while men were more likely to search for another job and therefore continue to be counted as members of the labor force.[20] Women's lower unemployment rate also might have been associated with "less unemployment in the clerical and service occupations in which women predominate, and because women tend to secure jobs formerly held by men."[21]

Age

The increase in unemployment was greatest among young workers. As shown in Table 4, the number of unemployed 14 to 24 year olds rose by 251% between 1930 and 1940. Since the younger members of this group often are leaving school and looking for their initial jobs, one would expect them to encounter more unemployment than other labor force participants. Additionally, their lack of experience could make it difficult to find another job once laid off. As previously mentioned, the then recently enacted Fair Labor Standards Act (which prohibited 14- and 15-year-olds from working for manufacturers) effectively limited the job options of the very youngest workers as well.

Among workers age 25 and above, persons between 45 and 64 years old suffered the largest increase in unemployment. Although the Census Bureau did not calculate separate figures for workers age 55 to 64, it speculated that such data would reveal a greater proportion of unemployment in the older subset than among those age 45 to 54.[22] This speculation was borne out by two special state censuses of unemployment. In Michigan in 1935, 16.8% of employable persons age 45 to 49 and 19.5% of those age 50 to 54 were unemployed in contrast with 23.0% of employables age 55 to 59 and 27.3% of those age 60 to 64.[23] (Employables were defined as persons either employed or looking for work.) Similarly, in Massachusetts in 1934, between 22.0% and 23.3% of employables age 45 to 54 were jobless compared to between 26.0% and 30.0% of those age 55 to 64.[24]

The Census Bureau noted that the comparatively low unemployment rates of workers age 65 and older

> cannot be interpreted to mean that employment opportunities were most favorable for aged persons. Workers who lose their jobs at ages over 65 tend to retire from the labor force rather than undertake new enterprises or to search for jobs in competition with younger workers.[25]

Race

Although data on minority workers was very limited, it appears that black workers made up a disproportionate share of unemployed persons. In January 1934, for example, blacks comprised just 1.2% of all employables in Massachusetts, but 33.2% of employable blacks did not have jobs. In contrast, many fewer employable whites were unemployed (19.0%) despite their accounting for virtually all employables in the state (98.8%).[26] Similarly, based on a 19-city survey conducted in 1931, black women were a larger proportion of all unemployed women in each city than they were of all gainful women workers in each city. The converse was true among white women.[27]

The rate of increase in unemployment among blacks also was greater than among whites. Between February 1929 and February 1930, for example, there was an 8% rise in joblessness among usually gainfully employed black men in

Baltimore compared to a 2% rise among white men. Similarly, unemployment among black women in Baltimore climbed 13% compared to 7% among white women in the one-year period. [28]

The greater impact of the Depression on older men appears to have been compounded for black men. Once laid off, they were "at a disadvantage [in the labor market] on account of their age and on account of their race."[29]

Occupational and IndustryCharacteristics

Lower skilled workers were more adversely affected by the Depression than higher skilled workers. For example, while semiskilled workers represented 16.5% of gainful workers in 1930, they accounted for a larger share of all unemployed persons (25.3%) in 1937.[30] Nonfarm laborers similarly were greatly overrepresented among the unemployed. In contrast, farmers and other proprietors, managers, and officials as well as professional and clerical workers were underrepresented among the unemployed compared to their presence among gainful workers. (See **Table 5**.)

Table 4. Unemployment by Gender and Age, 1930 and 1940 (numbers in thousands)

Gender and Age	Number Unemployed		Unemployment Rate	
	1930	1940	1930	1940
Men	2,011	6,185	5.4%	15.4%
14-19 years	220	867	7.9	33.1
20-24 years	338	1,074	7.1	21.3
25-44 years	846	2,361	4.8	12.5
45-64 years	528	1,698	5.2	14.2
65 years and over	79	185	4.4	10.0
Women	440	1,776	4.2	13.6
14-19 years	146	434	9.2	31.1
20-24 years	94	425	4.1	15.8
25-44 years	140	592	3.2	9.7
45-64 years	56	307	3.0	12.0
65 years and over	4	18	1.6	6.5

Source: U.S. Bureau of the Census, *Sixteenth Census of the United States: 1940, Population: Estimates of Labor Force, Employment and Unemployment in the United States, 1940 and 1930*, Washington, DC, 1944.

Notes: The Census Bureau adjusted the data from the 1930 census to accord with labor force definitions utilized in the 1940 census. The Bureau did not adjust estimates by race.

Table 5. Distribution of the Unemployed by Occupation in 1937 and the Distribution of Gainful Workers by Occupation in 1930 (15-74 year olds)

Occupation	Unemployed Workers	Gainful Workers
Total	100.0%	100.0%
Professionals	3.4	6.1
Farmers (owners and tenants)	2.5	12.2
Other proprietors, managers, and officials	1.4	7.5
Clerical, sales and related workers	14.0	16.4
Skilled workers and supervisors	14.6	13.0
Semiskilled workers	25.3	16.5
Nonfarm laborers	19.9	12.9
Farm laborers	10.8	8.4
Servants	8.1	6.9

Source: U.S. Office of Administrator of the Census of Partial Employment, Unemployment, and Occupations, *Final Report on Total and Partial Unemployment, 1937*, vol. I, Washington, D.C., 1938.

Notes: The 1930 decennial census provided the latest nationwide count of gainful workers to which the 1937 count of unemployed workers could be compared. (See the Appendix for the definition of gainful workers.) The two also used the same occupational classification system. To attain age comparability between the 1937 unemployment registration and the 1930 census, the U.S. Office of the Administrator adjusted the census data to remove persons under age 15 and over age 74. The number of unemployed persons in 1937 includes public emergency workers and excludes new workers and workers who did not report an occupation.

The manufacturing, services, and construction industries accounted for a majority (63%) of all unemployed persons in 1937.[31] In 1937, 29% of all jobless persons formerly worked for manufacturers, with nearly one-fourth having been employed by iron and steel producers. Another 12% had worked in textile industries and 10% in clothing industries. Service-related firms (e.g., recreation and amusement, hotels, restaurants, and professional services) accounted for almost 18% of the unemployed. Some 16% of jobless persons were formerly employed in the construction industry.

Duration of Unemployment

Very long spells of unemployment were common during the 1930s. Among unemployed men in Massachusetts in January 1934, for example, 62% had been without jobs a year or longer while 45% had not worked in two or more years, 25% in three or more years, and 11% in the previous four or more years.[32] Women in the state fared slightly better with 54% unemployed a year or longer; 35%, two or more years; 18%, three or more years; and 8%, four or more years.

Table 6. Unemployment Rates by Region and State, 1940

Region by State	Unemployment Rate	Region by State	Unemployment Rate
New England	10.6%	Georgia	5.3%
Connecticut	8.7	Maryland	7.4
Maine	11.8	North Carolina	5.4
Massachusetts	11.2	South Carolina	4.0
New Hampshire	10.3	Virginia	6.4
Rhode Island	12.3	West Virginia	11.2
Vermont	7.2	*East South Central*	7.2
Middle Atlantic	13.6	Alabama	6.6
New Jersey	11.4	Kentucky	9.6
New York	13.7	Mississippi	4.8
Pennsylvania	14.4	Tennessee	7.3
East North Central	9.0	*West South Central*	8.3
Illinois	9.1	Arkansas	6.9
Indiana	8.0	Louisiana	8.1
Michigan	9.4	Oklahoma	10.2
Ohio	9.5	Texas	8.1
Wisconsin	8.4	*Mountain*	10.2
West North Central	8.0	Arizona	11.0
Iowa	6.4	Colorado	9.5
Kansas	7.3	Idaho	10.2
Minnesota	10.0	Montana	10.3
Missouri	8.5	Nevada	8.9
Nebraska	6.8	New Mexico	12.1
North Dakota	7.2	Utah	10.1
South Dakota	6.4	Wyoming	8.7
South Atlantic	6.5	*Pacific*	10.3
Delaware	7.6	California	10.6
District of Columbia	7.2	Oregon	9.7
Florida	7.6	Washington	9.9

Source: U.S. Bureau of the Census, *Sixteenth Census of the United States: 1940, Population: Comparative Occupation Statistics for the United States,* 1870 to 1940, Washington, D.C., 1943.

Long periods of unemployment remained prevalent later in the decade as well. Of the 4.7 million unemployed persons who reported the number of weeks they had worked during the preceding 12 months, 31% had been jobless for more than one year as of November 1937.[33] Even in 1940, after the Great Depression had ended, workers still were experiencing extended periods of unemployment. Of unemployed workers who reported when they were last employed, one-third had not held a job in a year or more.[34]

GeographicCharacteristics

Although it is unlikely that any geographic area was not touched by the Depression, some areas felt it more than others. In 1940, the Middle Atlantic region reported the highest rate of unemployment (13.6%) and two states within it—Pennsylvania (14.4%) and New York (13.7%)—had the highest jobless rates in the nation. In New England, which had the next highest unemployment rate (10.6%), every state except Connecticut and Vermont reported double-digit rates. Both the Pacificand Mountain regions also reported over one-tenth of their workers unemployed. (See Table 6.)

At the other end of the spectrum, the South Atlantic region had the lowest unemployment rate in the nation. On a state-by-state basis, South Carolina (4.0%) in the South Atlantic region and Mississippi (4.8%) in the East South Central region reported the lowest unemployment rates.

The number of workers laid off from manufacturing industries was large, the particular industries varying by region.[35] In New England, for example, there were substantial layoffs in the shoe, textile, and steel manufacturing industries. In the Middle Atlantic region, job losses were high at clothing, textile, and steel manufacturers. Layoffs were prevalent in the steel and auto industries of the East North Central region.

Farming, a major source of jobs at the time, accounted for much of the unemployment in other regions. They were the South Atlantic, East South Central, West South Central, West North Central, and Mountain regions.

In summary, about one in every four workers in the nation was unemployed in the worst year of the Great Depression. Many workers were unemployed for much longer than one year. Of those fortunate to have jobs, many experienced cutbacks in hours, and hence, earnings. Men—particularly those older and black—were among the most adversely affected during a time when age- and race-based employment discrimination were not unlawful and when occupational shifts in labor demand were operating against them. Lower skilled workers were at a greater disadvantage in the labor market than higher skilled workers. Those who toiled on farms and in factories were displaced in especially large numbers. And, states whose economies were dependent upon agriculture and manufacturing reported comparatively high unemployment rates.

COMPARISONWITH THE RECESSION THAT BEGAN IN DECEMBER 2007

The following analysis compares the Great Depression with the eleventh recession of the post-World War II period. It utilizes, when possible, seasonally adjusted monthly data for December 2007 (the recession's start) and the latest month in 2009 for which data are available. In those cases in which the U.S. Bureau of Labor Statistics (BLS) does not adjust monthly data for seasonal fluctuations, which prevents month-to-month comparisons, annual average data for 2008 are used. For the Depression period, data from tables earlier in the report are supplemented with data from the 1940 decennial census when it provides statistical series more akin to those available today.

From a labor market perspective, the eleventh recession in the post-World War II period is reminiscent in several respects of the Great Depression. The similarities are not unique to the two economic downturns, however. They are shared with many of the recessions that occurred in the intervening years. Analogously, the Great Depression differs from the latest and intervening recessions by having had a much worse effect on workers based on labor force measures (e.g., unemployment rate) and on the lack of a pre-existing safety net of government programs.

Similarities

There are a number of similarities between the characteristics of the unemployed during the Great Depression and the recession that began in December 2007. Three similarities are intertwined:

1. The cyclically sensitive goods-producing sector lays off workers during recessions in numbers that are out of proportion to the sector's share of total employment.[36]

2. The concentration of blue-collar occupations in the goods-producing sector means that workers in these jobs are particularly vulnerable to displacement during downturns in the business cycle.
3. Men, who dominate the ranks of workers in the goods-producing sector and in blue-collar occupations, typically are more adversely affected by recessions than women.

Workers in the mining, construction, and manufacturing industries are overrepresented among those who lose jobs during economic downturns. About 40% of nonfarm jobs during the Great Depression were in the goods-producing sector, but it accounted for 57% of all jobs cut from employer payrolls between 1929 and 1933 and 77% between 1937 and 1938.[37] By 2008, the goods-producing sector's share of nonfarm employment had fallen to 15.6%. Nonetheless, 50.4% of employees who lost jobs between December 2007 and May 2009 formerly worked in the mining, construction, and manufacturing industries.[38]

Workers in blue-collar occupations historically have accounted for a majority of employment in the cyclically sensitive goods-producing sector. In 1940, 66.1% of craft workers, operatives, and nonfarm laborers were employed in the mining, construction, and manufacturing industries.[39] The same holds true, albeit to a lesser extent, today: 51.1% of persons employed in construction and extraction occupations (e.g., craft workers, laborers) and in production occupations (e.g., machine operators, assemblers) work in the mining, construction and manufacturing industries.[40] As a result, workers in blue-collar occupations are at a higher than average risk of displacement during recessions.[41]

The greater concentration of men in cyclically sensitive industries and occupations contributes to the more adverse impact of recessions on male members of the labor force. One means of measuring this differential effect is to examine the trend in employment by gender. During the Great Depression, the number of employed women increased while the number of employed men decreased.[42] In 1940, men accounted for 94.3% of persons employed in the mining industry, 98.3% of those in the construction industry, and 78.0% of workers in the manufacturing industry.[43] In that year, men also composed 97.9% of craft workers, 96.8% of nonfarm laborers, and 75.2% of operatives and related workers.[44] Seven decades later, men remain the dominant jobholders in the goods-producing sector: in 2008, men accounted for

87.2% of employment in mining, 90.3% in construction, and 70.7% in manufacturing.[45] Last year, men also composed 97.5% of workers in construction and extraction occupations (e.g., craft workers, laborers) and 70.3% workers in production occupations (e.g., machine operators, assemblers).[46] Partly as a result, men's employment overall fell precipitously—by 5.4% (4.3 million)—from 78.3 million in December 2007 to 74.0 million in May 2009. Despite their somewhat increased presence over time in these industries and occupations, women experienced substantially less job loss than men during the current recession. The number of employed women fell 2.2% (1.5 million) from 68.0 million in December 2007 to 66.5 million in May 2009.[47]

The comparatively worse impact of recessions on male employment is not limited to the Great Depression and the recession that began in December 2007. According to an analysis conducted in 1993 of data from the Current Employment Statistics program, which began to collect data by gender in 1964, most of those who lost jobs in the five recessions that occurred between December 1969 and March 1991 were men. The researchers found that although women lost jobs in the last two of the five recessions covered by their analysis, men lost 9 to 19 times more jobs than women in the July 1990-March 1991 and July 1981-November 1982 recessions, respectively. They concluded that

> [t]he chief explanation for the vast differences in employment loss between women and men in recessions concerns the proportions of jobs held by women in the various industries.... [B]ecause the goods-producing industries bear most of the job loss during recessions and because employment in this sector is heavily male, men lose the great majority of jobs in recessions. The industry divisions that fare best during recessions, services and government, have a high concentration of women, partially accounting for women's relative job stability."[48]

The more negative effect of the Great Depression and recent recessions on male members of the labor force also is discernible from unemployment statistics. As was the case during the Depression,[49] unemployed men as a proportion of the male labor force exceeded unemployed women as a proportion of the female labor during the last three recessions. At the end of the 1981-1982 recession in November, the unemployment rate among men measured 11.1% compared to 10.2% among women; at the end of the 1990-1991 recession in March, the male unemployment rate was 7.2% compared to a female unemployment rate of 6.3%; and at the end of the 2001 recession in November, the unemployment rate for men measured 5.7% compared to 5.4% for women. Similarly, in May 2009, 17 months into the latest recession, men's unemployment rate was 10.5% as opposed to women's unemployment rate of 8.0%.[50]

Research also suggests that varying trends in the growth rates of male- and female-dominated industries contributed to the relatively worse unemployment experience of men starting with the 1981-82 recession.[51] More specifically, it was estimated that faster employment growth in industries with large concentrations of women compared to industries with large concentrations of men narrowed the female-male unemployment differential to the point where men's unemployment rate exceeded that of women during recent recessions—in stark contrast with the comparative level of their unemployment rates during most of the post-World War II period.

4. Lower-skilled workers are more susceptible to unemployment than higher-skilled workers.

   The incidence of unemployment tends to vary inversely with the skill level of a worker (regardless of the stage of the business cycle).[52] In 1940, the unemployment rate among craft workers (13.7%) and nonfarm laborers (19.5%) was substantially higher than the unemployment rate among professionals (2.4%) and nonfarm proprietors, managers, and officials (2.0%), for example.[53] Unemployment rates by occupation show the same pattern today. The unemployment rate of workers in management, professional, and related occupations (2.7%) was well below the rate of natural resources, construction, and maintenance occupations (8.8%) and production occupations (7.7%) in 2008.[54]

   Looking at the data in terms of changes in employment reveals the same pattern: higher-skilled workers weather economic downturns better than lower-skilled workers on average. Between 1930 and 1940, employment among professionals and nonfarm proprietors, managers, and officials increased.[55] Similarly, between 2007 and 2008, employment of comparatively high-skilled workers increased by 973,000 among management, professional and related occupations.[56] In contrast, employment among craft workers and nonfarm laborers decreased during the Depression period. Employment of workers in construction and extraction occupations and in production occupations decreased as well between 2007 and 2008, falling by 934,000 and 422,000, respectively.

5. Once unemployed, older workers have a more difficult time becoming reemployed.

> The high proportion of workers under 25 years old who were unemployed at the time of the [1940] census were due to a comparatively rapid turnover in employment, with frequent but relatively short periods of idleness. Among workers 55 to 64 years old, on the other hand, unemployment apparently occurred less frequently, but those who lost their jobs experienced relatively great difficulty in finding another job, and tended to remain unemployed for comparatively long periods.[57]

In 1940, the median duration of unemployment was about seven months for job seekers up to age 35. The length of unemployment spells increased for each age group thereafter.[58]

The pattern of older workers having more difficulty finding new jobs has recurred. In 2008, the median duration of unemployment for all workers was 9.4 weeks as opposed to 12.2 weeks for 45 to 54 year olds and 11.8 weeks for 55 to 64 year olds.[59] Jobless workers age 45 and older also were overrepresented among the long-term unemployed (i.e., those without jobs for at least six months). While 28.5% of all unemployed workers were at least 45 years old, these baby-boom generation workers accounted for 37.8% of the long-term unemployed.

As was the case during the Depression, some speculate that age discrimination plays a role in the reemployment problems of today's older workers. For example, the publisher of a job listing website (Workforce50.com) recently asserted that older workers suffer from a misperception among employers of "being overqualified, overpriced, technologically challenged and inflexible."[60] "Many out-of-work baby boomers have despaired as they wonder whether to trim their resumes to avoid giving away their decades of work experience, or to dye their hair."[61] A report by the House Select Committee on Aging offered age discrimination as one explanation for the reemployment difficulties of older workers during the steep 1981-1982 recession, when the national unemployment rate last broke 10%.[62]

6. The number of people involuntarily working part-time increases during economic downturns.

   Just as involuntary part-time employment increased during the 1930s, so too has it grown today. The number of persons working part-time for economic reasons, that is, who would prefer full-time jobs if they were available, almost doubled in nonfarm industries between December 2007 and May 2009, from 4,548,000 to 8,928,000.[63]

Differences

In Magnitude

There are substantial differences in the extent of unemployment during the Great Depression and the current recession. The unemployment rate rose almost eight-fold between 1929 (3.2%) and 1933 (24.9%). In contrast, it almost doubled between December 2007 (4.9%) and May 2009 (9.4%). At the peak of unemployment during the Great Depression (1933), one in four workers was unemployed, in contrast with fewer than one in eleven today. To approximate the pervasiveness of unemployment at the depth of the Depression, the number of workers without jobs would have to have totaled 38.6 million in May 2009, which is 24 million more workers than were unemployed this May (14.5 million).[64]

Employers cut the total number of jobs on their payrolls much more deeply during the Great Depression than they have thus far in the latest recession. Between 1929 and 1933, employment on nonfarm payrolls fell by 24.3%, compared to 4.3% thus far in the recession. To approximate the relative extent of cutbacks that took place over the four-year period between 1929 and 1933, employers would have had to have shed 27.6 million more workers than they did between December 2007 and May 2009. In the goods-producing sector, 7.2 million rather than 3.0 million workers would have to have been laid off since the recession began to equal the relative impact of the four-year (1929-1933) decline. Within the goods-producing sector, construction companies would have had to have pared payrolls by 2.2 million more jobs than the 1.2 million positions cut through May 2009. Manufacturers would have had to have let go 2.5 million workers beyond the 1.8 million they displaced since December 2007 if the industry was in as relatively bad shape as it was in 1933.[65]

A comparison between these labor force measures two years into the Depression and thus far in the ongoing recession similarly shows the latter to be less severe than the former. By 1931, the unemployment rate had risen to 15.9% or five times higher than the 3.2% recorded in 1929.[66] In contrast, the unemployment rate almost doubled 17 months into the latest recession (going from 4.9% in December 2007 to 9.4% in May 2009).[67] To approximate the pervasiveness of unemployment in 1931, the number of workers without jobs would have to have totaled 24.7 million in May 2009, which is 10 million more workers than were unemployed in that month.

Similarly, the 4.3% decrease in nonfarm payroll employment 17 months into the recession compares favorably with the 15.0% decrease recorded two years into the Depression.[68] To approximate this difference in job loss, employers would have had to have let go 14.7 million more workers than they did between December 2007 and May 2009. In the goods-producing sector, 5.0 million rather than 3.0 million workers would have to have been laid off since the current recession began to equal the relative impact of the 1929-1931 decline. Within the goods-producing sector, construction companies would have had to have pared payrolls by 1.4 million jobs rather than the 1.2 million positions eliminated through May 2009. Manufacturers would have had to have shed almost 1.5 million workers beyond the 1.8 million displaced since December 2007 if the industry was performing as badly as it had two years into the Depression.

Geographically

At least part of the different effect by geographic area of the Great Depressionand current recession flows from the industry composition of states. As shown in Table 7, many of the states in the East North Central region had among the highest unemployment rates in May 2009 (the latest month for which state data are available). The difficulties of the area, whose employment base remains heavily dependent upon goods production,[69] reflect the current recession's intensification of the long-term problems of U.S. manufacturers—particularly those companies that directly and indirectly employ many of the region's workers at auto assembly plants and parts suppliers.[70] In contrast, the Middle Atlantic and New England regions reported the highest unemployment rates in 1940.[71] The comparatively better unemployment picture in these regions during the current recession likely is associated with diversification of their employment away from manufacturing industries (e.g., shoe, clothing, and textile production) over the past several decades.[72]

Table 7. Unemployment Rates by Region and State, May 2009

Region by State	Unemployment Rate	Region by State	Unemployment Rate
New England	8.3%	Maryland	7.2
Connecticut	8.0	North Carolina	11.1
Maine	8.3	South Carolina	12.1
Massachusetts	8.2	Virginia	7.1
New Hampshire	6.5	West Virginia	8.6
Rhode Island	12.1	*East South Central*	10.3
Vermont	7.3	Alabama	9.8
Middle Atlantic	8.3	Kentucky	10.6
New Jersey	8.8	Mississippi	9.6
New York	8.2	Tennessee	10.7
Pennsylvania	8.2	*West South Central*	7.0
East North Central	11.0	Arkansas	7.0
Illinois	10.1	Louisiana	6.6
Indiana	10.6	Oklahoma	6.3
Michigan	14.1	Texas	7.1
Ohio	10.8	*Mountain*	7.8
Wisconsin	8.9	Arizona	8.2
West North Central	7.3	Colorado	7.6
Iowa	5.8	Idaho	7.8
Kansas	7.0	Montana	6.3
Minnesota	8.2	Nevada	11.3
Missouri	9.0	New Mexico	6.5
Nebraska	4.4	Utah	5.4
North Dakota	4.4	Wyoming	5.0
South Dakota	5.0	*Pacific*	11.1
South Atlantic	9.6	Alaska	8.4
Delaware	8.1	California	11.5
District of Columbia	10.7	Hawaii	7.4
Florida	10.2	Oregon	12.4
Georgia	9.7%	Washington	9.4

Source: U.S. Bureau of Labor Statistics, data from the Local Area Unemployment Statistics program.

Another reason for the different geographic effect of the Great Depression and the current recession is the varying impact of the two downturns in nonmanufacturing industries. Many states that were dependent on the agricultural industry suffered greatly during the 1930s. The unemployment rates of states from which farmers migrated (e.g., Oklahoma, Kansas, Texas, New Mexico, and Arkansas) might otherwise have been higher, while those migrants who were unable to find work might have raised the unemployment rates of agricultural states to which they were attracted (e.g., Arizona, California, Idaho, Oregon, and Washington).[73] In the current recession, states whose growth had been fueled in part by other nonmanufacturing industries—construction and real estate services—had double-digit unemployment rates in May 2009 (e.g., California, Nevada and Oregon; see Table 7.).[74] Contributing to the comparatively poor labor market conditions in the two Pacific states and in North Carolina, among other states, is their reliance on industries that did not even exist in the 1930s, such as high-tech, with enterprises located in California's Silicon Valley, Oregon's Silicon Forest, and North Carolina's Research Triangle.[75]

In the Impact of BeingUnemployed

The implications of being unemployed have changed substantially over time. One reason for the altered situation facing jobless persons is the increased prevalence of families in which both spouses work. In 1940, three-fifths of married-couple families reported the husband as sole breadwinner.[76] In 2008, the husband was the lone earner in about one-fifth of married-couple families. Both spouses were employed in another 51.4% of married-couple families.[77] Consequently, the financial impact of joblessness is likely to be less today than it was more than half a century ago, when unemployment more often meant the total absence of a paycheck for a larger proportion of families.

Even for those persons who were employed during the Great Depression, the dismal economy created a greater hardship than is the case today because of the much deeper drop in earnings and hours worked. Average hourly earnings of factory workers in manufacturing industries fell by 21.4% between 1929 and 1933 and by 8.9% between 1929 and 1931. In addition, average weekly hours for these workers decreased by 13.8% between 1929 and 1933 and by 8.4% between 1929 and 1931.[78] As of May 2009, in contrast, average hourly earnings of nonmanagerial workers in manufacturing industries decreased by 3.9% and their hours by 5.6%.[79]

Another important difference between the Great Depression and the current recession, in terms of the economic hardship inflicted by high unemployment, is the nationwide availability of public assistance programs in place today. Before the 1930s, public assistance was provided by private charities and local governments.[80] State governments did not become involved in the provision of public relief until the latter part of 1931, as it became increasingly apparent that the traditional sources of assistance could not meet the rising needs of unemployed workers and their families. Seven states (New York, New Jersey, Wisconsin, Pennsylvania, Rhode Island, Illinois, and Ohio) appropriated and distributed unemployment relief between September 1931 and July 1932. Following passage of the Emergency Relief and Construction Act of 1932 by Congress, 33 more states became involved in providing public assistance. The act was the only major federal measure passed during the Hoover Administration explicitly to aid the jobless. It came almost four years after the Depression began.

The Emergency Relief and Construction Act was signed reluctantly by President Hoover, who believed that the traditional sources of relief were the most appropriate agencies to handle the needs of the unemployed. The act was envisioned as a temporary measure, not to imply long-term commitment of federal resources in this area. The federal money was offered to the states in the form of loans that were to be repaid with interest or through deductions from future federal aid to states for highways. (This repayment feature was cancelled by Congress in 1938 during the Roosevelt Administration.)

Not until enactment of the Federal Emergency Relief Act of 1933 (FERA) during the Roosevelt Administration did the federal government truly commit its own resources for provision of assistance to the unemployed. FERA, through matching grants and discretionary funds under Title I, aided employable persons and their dependents with cash and in-kind benefits between 1933 and 1935. Even under this program, however, direct public relief was considered a temporary measure ("the dole"), while work relief (job creation) programs were emphasized.

With passage of the Social Security Act in 1935—two years after the end of the Depression period's first downturn—the federal government established a permanent presence in the area of benefit transfer programs (e.g., old-age and survivors insurance, unemployment insurance). Thus, persons unemployed during the current recession did not have to wait until controversy ended over whether aid should be administered by private or public agencies, until state governments and the federal government awoke to the magnitude of the jobless problem and intervened, or until an administrative system was established at the state and federal levels before they received benefits.

In addition to already having safety net programs in place to cushion the impact of unemployment, today's jobless also benefit more from the social legislation than did the Depression's unemployed. A nationwide federal-state unemployment compensation program was part of the original Social Security Act, but when it was enacted, many groups were excluded from coverage.

Among the excluded were workers in government and educational organizations as well as those laid off from small firms. As a result, the unemployment compensation program covered less than half of all employees in 1940.[81] Over the years, the system has been expanded so that today almost all wage and salary workers are covered.[82]

Workers eligible for unemployment compensation (UC) during the current recession also collect benefits for a longer period of time than persons unemployed during the Depression. In December 1937, for example, 12 states provided benefits for a maximum of 12-14 weeks; 33 states, 15-17 weeks; and 4 states, 18-20 weeks.[83] Most states now provide regular UC benefits for a maximum of 26 weeks. There is a permanently authorized extended benefit program in effect today as well that provides an additional 13 or 26 weeks of UC benefits in high-unemployment states. In addition, the 110th Congress authorized as part of P.L. 110-252 a temporary unemployment benefit program for workers in all states who exhausted their regular benefits. The 111th Congress extended the temporary program and expanded upon it in the American Recovery and Reinvestment Act of 2009 (P.L. 111-5).[84]

Yet another liberalization of the law since the 1930s that helps today's unemployed workers involves the waiting period before benefits can be collected. In the early years of the system, states had waiting periods ranging from two to four weeks.[85] Currently, 25 states have no waiting period and the remaining states have a one-week requirement.[86]

Moreover, in the Emergency Unemployment Compensation Amendments of 1992 (P.L. 102-318), a work-sharing program was authorized permanently. It allows employers who temporarily cutback the hours of their employees rather than laying them off to develop short-time compensation plans. If the plans are approved by the state in which the firms are located, employees involuntarily working reduced schedules can receive partial UC benefits.[87] No program to compensate workers for the wage losses associated with pervasive involuntary part-time employment existed during the Great Depression.

Finally, the UC system was of no value to jobless workers during the Depression period's first economic downturn as the Social Security Act was not passed until 1935. In addition, no benefits were paid out for the first two years in order for reserve funds to accumulate.[88] It also was of no value to those who were jobless for so long during the 1930s that they did not meet the earnings or work time criteria for eligibility.

Other federal programs available to assist those persons unemployed today also were in their infancy during the 1930s. In September 1933, it became national policy to provide aid to farmers and the unemployed by purchasing the farmers' surplus produce and distributing it to the unemployed and their families. However, because of problems with the commodity distribution program, a new idea – food stamps – emerged in the late 1930s. The first food stamps were purchased in Rochester, New York in May 1939. Before the program ended in March 1943, it operated in half the counties of the nation. Thus, although food was available to the unemployed and their dependents in some geographic areas during the Depression, both the commodity distribution and food stamp programs did not start until after the economic downturns of the 1930s had ended.[89]

APPENDIX. THE EVOLUTION OF LABOR FORCE DATA

During the past several decades, the definition and measurement of employment and unemployment have undergone many changes. The data available during the Great Depression are first described below. Next, the data available today are contrasted with the Depression-era statistics.

The Great Depression

Between the 1930 and 1940 censuses, the Census Bureau went from the gainful worker to labor force concept. Up to and including the 1930 census, individuals aged *10* and above reported themselves as gainful workers if they had *at some time* worked in an occupation in which they earned money or the equivalent, or in which they assisted in the production of marketable goods – *regardless of their activity at the time of the census*. Thus, persons who had never worked but were available for work were not counted as gainful workers. Beginning with the 1940 census, individuals aged *14* and above reported themselves as members of the labor force if they were employed for pay or profit, or at unpaid family work, *during the week of March 24 to 30, 1940*, or were seeking jobs or performing public emergency work during the specified period. The changeover from a gainful worker to labor force concept raised the age criteria, included new workers, and specified a time period in which labor market activity must have occurred. It also created discrepancies between the two census counts in the way other individuals were classified (e.g., seasonal workers, inmates of institutions, retired and disabled persons).[90] The Census Bureau's adjustment of the gainful worker concept to the labor force concept produced a net decrease of 1.2 million persons in the figure for gainful workers reported in the 1930 census.

The second change was in the measurement of unemployment. The 1930 census was the first national effort to count the unemployed. *Gainful workers* were asked if they had been at work *the day before* the census-taker called. If they were not at work, the individual was asked

> whether they had a job, whether they were able to work, whether they were looking for work, whether they had lost pay because they were not at work, and the reason for their idleness. On the basis of this information, gainful workers not at work "yesterday" were classified into the following seven categories: [91]

- were jobless, able to work, and looking for work;
- were on layoff without pay, excluding the sick and voluntarily idle;
- were jobless and unable to work;
- had a job but were idle due to sickness or disability;
- were jobless and not looking for work;
- had a job but were voluntarily idle without pay; or
- had a job and were being paid although not at work.

According to the definition of the labor force introduced in the 1940 census, however, an individual was classified as either employed if at work *within a given week,unemployed if seeking work or performing public emergency work within a given week,* or not in the labor force if neither of the prior two classifications applied. The Census Bureau adjusted the much broader definition of unemployment in the 1930 census to comply with that of the 1940 census by estimating for each of the seven categories the number of individuals who would have been classified as unemployed had the 1940 census definition been utilized. The Bureau also estimated for those not included in the gainful worker definition (e.g., new workers) the number of persons who would have been counted as unemployed. Of the 2,451,000 workers the Census Bureau estimated to be unemployed in 1930 based on the 1940 census definition, 213,000 were new workers and 2,238,000 were classified as experienced workers seeking jobs.

Several surveys of states and cities as well as the 1937 nationwide census of unemployment were conducted during the course of the Depression to gauge the pervasiveness of unemployment and the characteristics of the unemployed. The data sources were based on outdated (un)employmentconcepts and permit only a snapshot rather than time-series analysis as they were not conducted on a recurring basis. However, the sources were included in the preceding analysis because they provide data unavailable from the decennial censuses and data for intercensal years.

Today Compared to the Great Depression

When comparisons are made in the report between unemployment rates during the course of the Depression and recession, the Depression-era data are retrospective estimates designed to be comparable with the Current Population Survey (CPS) rather than the 1930 and 1940 decennial censuses.[92] Today, the CPS is the official source of timely labor force data. Its precursor was developed by the Works Progress Administration (WPA) in 1940. The Census Bureau assumed responsibility for the monthly unemployment report from the WPA in 1942.[93] In the late 1950s, the Bureau of Labor Statistics assumed responsibility for the content, analysis and release of labor force data derived from CPS which continues to be conducted by the Census Bureau. Based on the CPS, the Bureau of Labor Statistics releases estimates each month on the labor force status of individuals.

End Notes

1 For more information, see CRS Report R40007, *Financial Market Turmoil and U.S. Macroeconomic Performance*, by Craig K. Elwell; and CRS Report R40198, *U.S. Economy in Recession: Similarities To and Differences From the Past*, by Marc Labonte.

2 John E. Bregger, "The Current Population Survey: a Historical Perspective and BLS' Role," *Monthly Labor Review*, June 1984, p. 8.

3 U.S. Office of Administrator of the Census of Partial Employment, Unemployment, and Occupations, *Final Report on Total and Partial Unemployment, 1937*, vol. I, Washington, D.C., 1938, pp. VII-VIII.

4 For example, the Census Bureau's adjustment of the 1930 gainful worker concept to the 1940 labor force concept reduced the former by 1.2 million persons.

5 U.S. Bureau of the Census, *Sixteenth Census of the United States: 1940, Population: Comparative Occupation Statistics for the United States, 1870 to 1940*, Washington, D.C., 1943.

6 John D. Durand, *The Labor Force in the United States, 1890-1960* (New York: Social Science Research Council, 1948), pp. 114-115.

7 Ibid..

8 Ibid.

9 U.S. Bureau of the Census, *Sixteenth Census of the United States: 1940, Population: Comparative Occupation Statistics for the United Sates, 1870 to 1940*, Washington, D.C., 1943.

[10] Ibid.

[11] Although the "establishment survey" is limited to nonfarm employers, they have accounted for the majority of total U.S. employment since at least 1900. Annual estimates of employment that were developed retrospectively and appear in *Historical Statistics of the United States, Colonial Times to 1970* (U.S. Bureau of the Census, Washington, D.C., 1975) show that nonfarm employees composed 77% of total U.S. employment in 1929 for example.

[12] U.S. Bureau of Labor Statistics, *Employment, Hours, and Earnings, United States, 1909-90*, Bulletin 2370, vol. I, Washington, D.C., 1991.

[13] Mitchell Broadus, "Depression Decade: From New Era to New Deal, 1929-1942," *in Economic History of the United States*, vol. IX (New York: Holt, Rhinehard, and Winston, 1962).

[14] Annual estimates of the number of employed and unemployed persons nationally and in the farm sector and nonfarm sector appear in U.S. Bureau of the Census, *Historical Statistics of the United States, Colonial Times to 1970* (Washington, D.C., 1975). These estimates are not available for the individual nonfarm industries shown in **Table 3**. They are not consistent with data from the decennial censuses and the establishment survey. The estimates were constructed retrospectively to be comparable with the Current Population Survey which was initiated in 1940.

[15] William J. Barrett, "Extent and Methods of Spreading Work," *Monthly Labor Review*, September 1932.

[16] Martin Nemirow, "Work-sharing Approaches: Past and Present," *Monthly Labor Review*, September 1984, p. 35.

[17] Ibid., pp. 35-36.

[18] U.S. Bureau of the Census, *Historical Statistics of the United States, Colonial Times to 1970* (Washington, D.C., 1975). These retrospectively constructed estimates are not consistent with data from the decennial censuses.

[19] Mitchell Broadus, "Depression Decade: From New Era to New Deal, 1929-1941," in *Economic History of the United States*, vol. IX (New York: Holt, Rinehart, and Winston, 1962).

[20] U.S. Bureau of the Census, *Sixteenth Census of the United States: 1940, Population: Estimates of the Labor Force, Employment, and Unemployment in the United States, 1940 and 1930*, Washington, D.C., 1944.

[21] Mitchell Broadus, "Depression Decade: From New Era to New Deal, 1929-1941," *in Economic History of the United States*, vol. IX (New York: Holt, Rinehart, and Winston, 1962), p. 98.

[22] U.S. Bureau of the Census, *Sixteenth Census of the United States: 1940, Population: Estimates of the Labor Force, Employment, and Unemployment in the United States, 1940 and 1930*, Washington, D.C., 1944.

[23] "Michigan Population and Unemployment Census, 1935," *Monthly Labor Review*, November 1936.

[24] "Census of Unemployment in Massachusetts," *Monthly Labor Review*, December 1934.

[25] U.S. Bureau of the Census, *Sixteenth Census of the United States: 1940, Population: Estimates of the Labor Force, Employment, and Unemployment in the United States, 1940 and 1930*, Washington, D.C., 1944, p. 3.

[26] "Census of Unemployment in Massachusetts," *Monthly Labor Review*, December 1934.

[27] "Unemployment Among Women in the Early Years of the Depression," *Monthly Labor Review*, April 1934.

[28] U.S. Bureau of Labor Statistics, "Surveys of Unemployment in Baltimore, 1928, 1929, and 1930," *Handbook of Labor Statistics*, Washington, D.C., 1931.

[29] John D. Durand, *The Labor Force in the United States, 1890-1960* (New York: Social Science Research Council, 1948), p. 115.

[30] The 1937 census of unemployment collected information from unemployed persons only. *The Final Report on Total and Partial Unemployment, 1973* compared its unemployment

estimates with data on gainful workers from the then most recent source of national data, namely, the 1930 census of population.

[31] U.S. Office of Administrator of the Census of Partial Employment, Unemployment, and Occupations, *Final Report on Total and Partial Unemployment, 1973*, vol. I, Washington, D.C., 1938.

[32] "Census of Unemployment in Massachusetts," *Monthly Labor Review*, December 1934.

[33] U.S. Office of Administrator of the Census of Partial Employment, Unemployment, and Occupations, *Final Report on Total and Partial Unemployment*, vol., I, Washington, D.C., 1938.

[34] U.S. Bureau of the Census, *Sixteenth Census of the United States: 1940, Population: The Labor Force*, Washington, D.C., 1943.

[35] U.S. Office of Administrator of the Census of Partial Employment, Unemployment, and Occupations, *Final Report on Total and Partial Unemployment*,, vol. I, Washington, D.C., 1938.

[36] The goods-producing sector is more sensitive to downturns in the business cycle than the service-providing sector because inventories of goods produced by the mining, construction and manufacturing industries build up due to reduced product demand during recessions. Firms in these industries consequently cut production and layoff workers as unsold homes and cars, for example, accumulate. Not until inventories diminish sufficiently do businesses increase production and not until they are confident that a sustained recovery is underway do firms (re)hire workers.

[37] Calculated from the data in **Table 3**.

[38] BLS, data from the Current Employment Statistics program, http://stats.bls.gov/ces.

[39] U.S. Bureau of the Census, *Sixteenth Census of the United States: 1940, Population: The Labor Force*, Washington, D.C., 1943.

[40] BLS, data from the Current Population Survey, http://stats.bls.gov/cps/cpsaat17.pdf.

[41] During the 2001-2002 period, which encompassed the 2001 recession, the rate of job loss among long-tenured workers previously employed in production occupations was 8.7% while the average displacement rate was a much lower 4.8%. (This is the latest recessionary period for which data are available from BLS' Displaced Worker Survey.) See the following report for additional information on the risk of displacement by occupation, industry, and other variables over time, CRS Report RL32292, Offshoring (a.k.a. *Offshore Outsourcing) and Job Insecurity Among U.S. Workers*, by Linda Levine.

[42] See **Table 1**.

[43] U.S. Bureau of the Census, *Sixteenth Census of the United States: 1940, Population: The Labor Force*, Washington, D.C., 1943.

[44] Ibid.

[45] BLS, data from the Current Population Survey, http://stats.bls.gov/cps/cpsaat17.pdf.

[46] BLS, data from the Current Population Survey, http://stats.bls.gov/cps/cpsaat11.pdf.

[47] BLS, data from the Current Population Survey, http://stats.bls.gov/cps.

[48] William Goodman, Stephen Antczak, and Laura Freeman, "Women and Jobs in Recessions: 1969-92," *Monthly Labor Review*, July 1993, p. 28-29.

[49] See **Table 4** for 1930 and 1940 unemployment rates by gender.

[50] BLS, data from the Current Population Survey, http://stats.bls.gov/cps.

[51] Larry DeBoer and Michael Seeborg, "The Female-Male Unemployment Differential: Effects of Changes in Industry Employment," *Monthly Labor Review*, November 1984, pp. 8-15.

[52] Often, occupational groups are used as proxies for skill level. An occupational group's comparative skill level is based on the predominant number of years of schooling completed by persons employed in the group. In 1940, for example, 68.1% of professional and related workers had attended or completed college as had 20.3% of nonfarm proprietors, managers and officials (except farm) and 18.4% of clerical, sales and related workers. In contrast, 35.1% of nonfarm laborers, 38.6% of operatives and related workers, and 41.7% of craft and related workers had at most completed the first seven or eight years of elementary

school. U.S. Bureau of the Census, *Sixteenth Census of the United States: 1940, Population: Comparative Occupation Statistics for the United States, 1870 to 1940*, Washington, D.C., 1943.

[53] U.S. Bureau of the Census, *Sixteenth Census of the United States: 1940, Population: The Labor Force*, Washington, D.C., 1943.

[54] BLS, data from the Current Population Survey, http://stats.bls.gov/cps/cpsaat25.pdf.

[55] See **Table 2**.

[56] BLS, data from the Current Population Survey, http://stats.bls.gov/cps.

[57] U.S. Bureau of the Census, *Sixteenth Census of the United States: 1940, Population: The Labor Force (Sample Statistics), Part I: General Characteristics*, Washington, D.C., 1943, p. 15.

[58] Ibid.

[59] BLS, data from the Current Population Survey, http://stats.bls.gov/cps/cpsaat31.pdf.

[60] Tiffany Hsu, "Older Jobless Workers Face Tough Prospects," Chicago Tribune, May 3, 2009.

[61] Michael Luo, "Longer Unemployment for Those 45 and Older," The New York Times, April 13, 2009.

[62] U.S. Congress, House Select Committee on Aging, *The Unemployment Crisis Facing Older Americans, 97th Cong., 2nd sess.*, October 8, 1982, Comm. Pub. No. 97-367 (Washington: GPO, 1982).

[63] BLS, data from the Current Population Survey, http://stats.bls.gov/cps.

[64] The analysis in this paragraph is based on depression-era data from *Historical Statistics of the United States, Colonial Times to 1970* (U.S. Bureau of the Census, Washington, D.C., 1975) and recent data from BLS, Current Population Survey.

[65] The analysis in this paragraph is based on depression-era data in BLS, *Employment, Hours, and Earnings, United States*, 1909-90, Bulletin 2370, vol. I, Washington, D.C., 1991, and data for later years from BLS, Current Employment Statistics program.

[66] U.S. Bureau of the Census, *Historical Statistics of the United States, Colonial Times to 1970* (Washington, D.C., 1975).

[67] BLS, data from the Current Population Survey.

[68] BLS, *Employment, Hours, and Earnings, United States, 1909-90*, Bulletin 2370, vol. I, Washington, D.C., 1991, and BLS, Current Employment Statistics program.

[69] In 2008, according to data from the Current Employment Statistics program, manufacturing jobs accounted for 11.1% of total nonfarm employment in Illinois, 17.7% in Indiana, 13.8% in Michigan and Ohio, and 17.2% in Wisconsin. The proportion in every state in the East North Central region was well above the average for the nation of 9.8% in 2008.

[70] Some states in other regions that are comparatively dependent on motor vehicle and parts manufacturing similarly have comparatively high unemployment rates (e.g., Kentucky, North Carolina, South Carolina, and Tennessee) as shown in **Table 7**. See also "Southeast Auto Parts Makers Feel Detroit's Pain," *MSN Money*, May 12, 2009.

[71] See **Table 6**.

[72] In 2008, according to data from the Current Employment Statistics program, manufacturing's share of total nonfarm employment in the Middle Atlantic region (7.9%) was well below the national average (9.8%). Specifically, the proportion in New Jersey was 7.4%; in New York, 6.1%; and in Pennsylvania, 11.1%. Manufacturing's share of total nonfarm employment in the New England region was equal to the national average of 9.8%. The shares of Maine (9.6%) and Massachusetts (8.7%) were below the average, while those of Connecticut (11.0%), New Hampshire (11.7%), Rhode Island (10.0%) and Vermont (11.4%) were above the average for the nation.

[73] See **Table 6**.

[74] Jennifer Robison, "Nevada Economy," *Las Vegas Review-Journal*, May 23, 2009; Peter Wong, "Is This Recession Oregon's Worst?," Statesman Journal, May 17, 2009; and Bob Willis, "California's Unemployment Rate Rises to 26-Year High," Bloomberg.com, March 20, 2009.

[75] "Recession Suddenly Humbles High-Tech Sector," *The Sacramento Bee*, May 24, 2009.

[76] U.S. Bureau of the Census, *Sixteenth Census of the United States: 1940, Population: Families, Employment Status*, Washington, D.C., 1943.

[77] BLS, *Employment Characteristics of Families in 2008*, Washington, D.C., May 27, 2009.

[78] BLS, *Employment, Hours, and Earnings, 1909-1990*, Bulletin 2370, vol. I, Washington, D.C., March 1991.

[79] BLS, data from the Current Employment Statistics program, http://www.bls.gov/ces/.

[80] Josephine C. Brown, *Public Relief 1929-1939* (New York: Henry Holt and Company, 1940).

[81] Tax Foundation Inc., *Unemployment Insurance: Trends and Issues*, Washington, D.C., 1982.

[82] According to the U.S. Department of Labor, 62% of unemployed workers in May 2009 received UC benefits from all programs operating at the time. For information on benefit receipt see the Unemployment Compensation chapter of the Committee on Ways and Means' *2008 Green Book* at http://waysandmeans.house.gov/media/pdf/111/uc.pdf.

[83] Paul A. Brinker, *Economic Insecurity and Social Security* (New York: Appleton-Century-Crofts, 1968).

[84] CRS Report RL33362, *Unemployment Insurance: Available Unemployment Benefits and Legislative Activity*, by Alison M. Shelton and Julie M. Whittaker.

[85] Tax Foundation, *Unemployment Insurance: Trends and Issues*, Washington, D.C., 1982.

[86] CRS Report RL33362, *Unemployment Insurance: Available Unemployment Benefits and Legislative Activity*, by Alison M. Shelton and Julie M. Whittaker.

[87] Short-time compensation programs exist in a minority of states today.

[88] Broadus Mitchell, "Depression Decade: From New Era to New Deal," in *Economic History of the United States* (New York: Holt, Rinehart, and Winston, 1962).

[89] U.S. Congress, House Committee on Agriculture, *Food Stamp Act of 1977*, 95th Cong., 1st sess., H.Rept. 95-464 (Washington: GPO, 1977).

[90] U.S. Bureau of the Census, *Sixteenth Census of the United States: 1940, Population: Estimates of the Labor Force, Employment, and Unemployment in the United States, 1940 and 1930*, Washington, D.C., 1944.

[91] U.S. Bureau of the Census, *Sixteenth Census of the United States: 1940, Population: Estimates of the Labor Force, Employment, and Unemployment in the United States*, 1940 and 1930, Washington, D.C., 1944, p. 2.

[92] The methodology utilized and resultant data from 1900 to 1947 appears in U.S. Bureau of the Census, *Historical Statistics of the United States, Colonial Times to 1970* (Washington, D.C., 1975).

[93] John E. Bregger, "The Current Population Survey: A Historical Perspective and BLS' Role," *Monthly Labor Review*, June 1984.

In: Recession, Depression, and Unemployment ISBN: 978-1-61761-508-5
Editors: Daniel A. García

Chapter 6

JOB CREATION PROGRAMS OF THE GREAT DEPRESSION: THE WPA AND THE CCC

Linda Levine

With the exception of the Great Depression, the recession that began in December 2007 is the nation's most severe according to various labor market indicators. The 7.1 million jobs cut from employer payrolls between December 2007 and September 2009, when it is thought the latest recession might have ended, is more than has been recorded for any postwar recession. Job loss was greater in a relative sense during the latest recession as well, recording a 5.1% decrease over the period.[1] In addition, long-term unemployment (defined as the proportion of workers without jobs for longer than 26 weeks) was higher in September 2009—at 36%—than at any time since 1948.[2]

As a result, momentum has been building among some members of the public policy community to augment the job creation and worker assistance measures included in the American Recovery and Reinvestment Act (P.L. 111-5). In an effort to accelerate improvement in the unemployment rate and job growth during the recovery period from the latest recession,[3] some policymakers recently have turned their attention to programs that temporarily created jobs for workers unemployed during the nation's worst economic downturn—the Great Depression—with which the latest recession has been compared.[4]

This chapter first describes the social policy environment in which the 1930s job creation programs were developed and examines the reasons for their shortcomings then and as models for current- day countercyclical employment measures. It then provides a brief overview of the two job creation programs of the Depression-era that Members of Congress have asked about most frequently: the Works Progress or Projects Administration (WPA)[5] and the Civilian Conservation Corps (CCC).

THEN AND NOW

At the outset of the Great Depression, the assistance government offered to unemployed workers and their families was in the form of direct relief. As recounted by Bremer based on historical documents, the provision of public assistance to workers displaced in the early years of the Depression entailed their first being

> subjected to means tests to prove their destitution, a procedure that [WPA Administrator] Hopkins described as fostering the "wholesale degradation of [their] finest sensibilities." Second, direct relief was given in kind, so that others prescribed what the unemployed should eat and wear. Finally, relief investigators intervened in the lives of the unemployed, telling them "where and how they should live... [and] how they should order their relationships within the family group, with their relatives, neighbors and friends." Viewed as charity, direct relief bore a stigma derived from the traditional assumption that workless people were personally responsible for their misfortunes and incapable of managing their own affairs.[6]

Reformers of the day sought to dispel the notion that those unemployed during the Great Depression were at fault for their situation, to restore their badly battered morale, and to maintain their skills while they were out-of-work for years in many cases. Advocates of the Roosevelt Administration's New Deal tried to achieve these objectives through congressional enactment of

- an unemployment insurance program so that workers could earn the right to cash benefits when they lost jobs through no fault of their own rather than having to rely solely on private charity and public assistance, and
- work relief (job creation) programs so that the unemployed could earn a cash wage from employment rather than remaining idle and

dependent on "the dole" (the caustic label then applied to public assistance).

But, the several work relief programs in effect during the Depression period[7] appear to have had difficulty maintaining the morale and skills of participants for two policy-related reasons. First, publicly funded projects were not permitted to compete for workers with private employers. Toward that end, the job creation programs typically paid wages so low as to not dissuade participants from accepting work in the private sector. As a result, the wages offered through these programs sometimes were inadequate to fully support workers' families; this left them still dependent on public assistance. Second, many participants were employed in jobs derisively called *make work, leaf raking,* or *shovel leaning* because "construction projects that might take business away from private contractors" were prohibited and government could not be involved "in the production, distribution, or sale of goods and services normally provided by private employers."[8] Such limitations made it difficult to develop worthwhile jobs, that is, jobs that boosted participants' morale and utilized skills they had acquired during prior employment.

The programs also were seemingly unable to employ a large proportion of unemployed workers due in part to their eligibility requirements and funding. Federal budget constraints were often invoked as a reason for limiting the funding of work relief programs. Even in the case of the comparatively well-funded WPA, appropriations typically were made annually in emergency acts and not adjusted upward to reflect later increases in unemployment. As a result, the largest of the job creation programs was unable to keep pace with increasing demand for public employment. For example, after the WPA's annual appropriation had been set, unemployment again began to rise in late 1937, and the percentage of unemployed persons in WPA jobs fell from about 30% to less than 20%.[9] Although part of the decline during the 1930s in the proportion of unemployed persons participating in the WPA can also be attributed to the development of other job creation programs and to the availability of unemployment insurance benefits starting in 1938, these measures did not assist a majority of unemployed workers even at the decade's end.

Work relief programs were not available to all unemployed persons, however. "Except for the short-lived Civil Works Administration and to a lesser extent the youth programs, employment on projects has been limited to unemployed persons in need."[10] In the case of the WPA specifically, public jobs were to be provided to *one unemployed person per family eligible for or receiving direct relief*.[11] Typically, local public assistance agencies certified the unemployed head of the needy family for WPA employment.

Although some might argue that the WPA's eligible population of one unemployed person per family was less limiting than it might appear because relatively few married women were members of the labor force in the 1 930s compared to today, the policy nonetheless suggests that demographic and other changes since then in the labor force (e.g., occupational composition) might lessen the suitability of Depression-era programs as models for current-day job creation programs. For example, laborers and semiskilled workers accounted for over one-half of all persons unemployed during the Depression.[12] Thus, they were a plentiful source of fitting candidates for the many low-skilled jobs created by WPA public works (construction) projects, and for the many physically demanding jobs of the CCC. Today, in contrast, perhaps one-fourth of the unemployed previously worked in comparable occupations.[13]

THE WPA

On January 4, 1935, President Roosevelt presented to Congress a plan for a federal works program. Congress in April authorized almost $4.9 billion in the Emergency Relief Appropriation (ERA) Act of 1935 (P.L. 74-11), with about $4.0 billion directed to the activities of the new works program.[14] Some $1.4 billion was allocated to the WPA, which President Roosevelt, acting under the authority of the ERA Act, established in Executive Order 7034 in May 1935. He charged the WPA with

- coordinating the activities of the works program—which was to provide temporary jobs through existing (the CCC and Public Works Administration) and new emergency public employment agencies established under the authority of the ERA Act (the Resettlement Administration and National Youth Administration) and numerous other federal agencies (the Bureau of Public Roads and Corps of Engineers)—and
- administering small-scale "useful projects" utilizing unemployed workers receiving or eligible for public assistance.[15]

However, the WPA's primary responsibility almost immediately became provision of employment on public works and public service projects rather than coordination of the overall program because most of the other federal agencies were able to provide little temporary employment.[16]

The WPA differed considerably from the Public Works Administration (PWA), with which it sometimes is confused. The public works (construction) projects of the WPA were intended to be quicker to start up, less costly, and more labor-intensive than those of the PWA. The WPA was to undertake construction projects (including repair and maintenance) costing less than $25,000, while the PWA was to undertake new construction projects costing more than $25,000.[17] The PWA operated almost completely by awarding grants to states, municipalities, and other public agencies, which in turn entered into contracts with private employers; this resembles the dissemination of much federal infrastructure spending today. In contrast, the WPA, by hiring participants onto the federal payroll, was able to ensure that jobs went to the needy unemployed.[18] With regard to the labor-intensity of WPA and PWA projects, it was estimated that an individual could be employed for one month on a WPA project for $82, on average, with the federal share being $63.50, while the cost of employing an individual for one month on a PWA project was estimated to average $330.[19] The WPA differed from the PWA as well by having a small public service component.

WPA employment ranged from fewer than 1.0 million persons as it started up in 1935, and as it wound down in 1942-1943, to a high of more than 3.3 million persons in November 1938.[20] The percentage of the unemployed who participated in WPA projects peaked at almost 40% in late 1936.[21]

For most of its existence, at least three-fourths of WPA employment involved public works projects of various types. More than one-half of this employment involved highway, road, and street construction. Three other types of projects accounted for about one-third of WPA public works employment: water and sewer systems and other public utilities, parks and other recreational facilities, and public buildings. The remaining temporary construction jobs were on conservation, sanitation, and airport projects. Except for the construction of public buildings, which required greater use of skilled workers, the majority of participants on WPA works projects were unskilled laborers and semiskilled factory workers.[22]

The public service component created jobs for less than one-fourth of WPA participants during most of the program's existence. Of the workers employed on service projects, most were engaged in so-called welfare activities (e.g., sewing and other goods production, feeding projects including school lunches, and public health work). Welfare activities provided employment largely to unskilled and semiskilled women workers. Research and records service projects (e.g., social and economic surveys, research assistance in publicly supported institutions of higher education), in contrast, accounted for most of the jobs that went to unemployed office and sales workers. Unemployed persons with professional and technical experience worked on so-called public activities service projects (e.g., educational services; library services; and music, art, writing, and theater projects).[23]

Although all persons employed by the WPA—from those who worked in headquarters, state, and local offices to those who worked on the program's projects—were federal employees, states and localities had a substantial role to play. Governmental agencies at state and local levels suggested projects to the WPA and managed their actual operation. After a sponsor developed a project plan in coordination with locally based WPA personnel, the plan was forwarded first to the state office staffed by WPA personnel and then to WPA headquarters for approval. An approved plan was

> returned to the state WPA office and may be put into operation at the discretion of the state administrator, who must plan his program in such a way that, within the limits of funds and employment quotas allotted to him, the various classes of needy workers in his area are kept regularly employed. ...State administrators have used various devices...to help solve the knotty problem as to which approved projects shall be given priority as opportunity presents itself. Frequently, however, the problem is not so much to choose among approved projects, as to find a sponsor to initiate a project needed to give employment. Failure of sponsors to initiate sufficient projects or those which will utilize special skills of white-collar or other workers, seriously hampers the WPA's effectiveness.[24]

Sponsors were required to contribute, either in cash or kind, to project costs. Their contributions principally went toward nonlabor costs and often made up a substantial share of total project costs. However, the variability across and within states in the share of project costs contributed by sponsors led Congress in the ERA Act of 1939 to set a minimum contribution for a state of 25% of the cost of all its projects. As part of their unsuccessful argument against the requirement, WPA officials stated that "Regardless of the amount of need in a given community, or of the desirability of a particular project, we cannot undertake it if it will reduce the average of all sponsors' participation [in a state] below 25 percent."[25]

Subject to the lobbying of Congress by business and labor groups, the WPA determined the wages, hours, and working conditions of program participants. As previously mentioned, firms did not want WPA wages set so high that project workers would be unwilling to accept jobs in the private sector.[26] Unions, for their part, were concerned about the potentially depressing impact WPA wages might have on those offered by companies.[27] The WPA developed a schedule of monthly earnings called "security wages" that was based on the skill level of jobs (unskilled, semiskilled, skilled, professional, and technical) and geographic area of employment. It also initially set a minimum range of hours to be worked each month by all workers on a project in order for them to earn their respective security wage. But, "it was pointed out that if skilled workers were required to work 140, or even 120, hours a month for security wages, their hourly rates would be below prevailing hourly rates, and this might lead to a lowering of hourly rates in private industry."[28] Congress consequently eliminated the uniform minimum hours requirement in 1936 by linking WPA wages to the prevailing hourly wage rate earned by workers in similar jobs in a locality. As a result, the number of hours worked by WPA participants on a given project varied greatly. The higher prevailing rate of skilled workers enabled them to earn their monthly security wage in many fewer hours than lesser skilled workers employed on the same project. Recognizing that the unequal hours of persons in different occupations working on the same project greatly hampered the efficiency of WPA operations, Congress in 1939 required that all project participants work 130 hours a month to earn their security wage. This effectively ended the WPA's prevailing wage policy.

THE CIVILIAN CONSERVATION CORPS

In March 1933, President Roosevelt proposed establishing a conservation corps "to be used in simple work, primarily confining itself to forestry, erosion, flood control, and related projects."[29] Secretary of Labor Frances Perkins testified at congressional hearings that the Administration regarded the program as a measure intended chiefly to help young single men who relief agencies had not considered because they were not a family's primary earner. That same month, Congress passed the Emergency Conservation Act (P.L. 73-5). It authorized the President to establish a program that would provide jobs to unemployed U.S. citizens in "the construction, maintenance, and carrying on of works of a public nature in connection with the forestation of lands..., the prevention of forest fires, floods, and soil erosion, plant pest and disease control, the construction, maintenance or repair of paths, trails and fire-lanes in the national parks and national forests..." The legislation further authorized the President by regulation to give program participants housing, clothing, health care, and a cash allowance. [30] The following month, the President created a conservation corps in Executive Order 6101 that came to be known as the CCC.

When Congress enacted the Civilian Conservation Corps Act of 1937 (P.L. 75-163), it put into statute many of the policies the Administration had developed through executive orders and other means in prior years. Most of the 300,000-enrollee-per-year cap set by Congress was meant to be filled by unemployed single male citizens aged 17 to 23.[31] The following groups could be enrolled regardless of marital status and age up to the stated levels: veterans, 30,000; Native Americans, 10,000; and residents of the territories, 5,000. Education of enrollees as a program objective was mentioned in statute for the first time: no less than 10 hours each week may be given over to general educational and vocational training.[32] In part because enrollees usually spent eight hours a day, five days a week working, the educational objective does not appear to have been well met.[33]

A director appointed by the President ran the CCC with the aid of an advisory council. The council was composed of the following federal agencies: the Departments of Agriculture, the Interior, Labor, and War, and the Veterans Administration. The director allocated the CCC's funds among the cooperating federal agencies. In FY1940, for example, more than 75% of the $278.8 million expended by the CCC was allotted to the War Department, 13% to the Agriculture Department, and 9% to the Interior Department.[34] The Labor Department relied on local relief agencies to certify the single young men for program enrollment.[35] The Veterans Administration selected enrollees from the population of eligible veterans. In the case of Native Americans, the Office of Indian Affairs in the Department of the Interior had total responsibility for all aspects of the program. [36]

The War Department housed, clothed, and otherwise oversaw the enrollees' welfare, including their education. The enrollees lived in camps that were usually built in isolated locations (e.g., national and state forests). There were approximately 2,000 camps, each of which housed about 200 persons. Individuals enrolled for a six-month period. Reenrollment was possible for additional six-month periods, subject to a two-year total limit.[37]

The Departments of Agriculture and the Interior were responsible for development and supervision of the work projects. The work projects fell into 10 general classifications:

1. structural improvements (e.g., fire towers, bridges, service buildings);
2. transportation improvements (e.g., truck trails, minor roads);
3. erosion control (e.g., check dams, terracing, vegetative covering);
4. flood control, irrigation, and drainage (e.g., dams, ditching);
5. forest culture (e.g., planting trees, seed collection);
6. forest protection (e.g., fire fighting, fire prevention);
7. landscape and recreation (e.g., public camp- and picnic-ground development);
8. range (e.g., elimination of predatory animals);
9. wildlife (e.g., stocking fish, food and cover planting);
10. miscellaneous (e.g., surveys, mosquito control).[38]

The Agriculture Department supervised the work projects of about three-fourths of the camps. More than half of these operated in national, state, or private forests and were under the direction of the Department's Forest Service. Of the minority of camps supervised by the Department of the Interior, most were under the direction of the National Parks Service; they performed functions similar to those of the forestry camps.[39]

"The vast range of CCC work was not performed without considerable cost. ...The annual cost per enrollee was $1,004, which compared unfavorably with that of the Works Progress Administration of $770 to $800, and the National Youth Administration of $400 to $700." It was asserted that the higher figure for the CCC should not be viewed in isolation from the individual and societal benefits that accrued from the corps' activities (e.g., improved health and morale of enrollees; money saved as a result of fire prevention work projects).[40] However, this can be said too with regard to the benefits of the WPA and the National Youth Administration. Although the emergency public employment agencies regularly compiled lists of their projects, calculations of the projects' economic value were rarely if ever published.[41]

The CCC appears to have been the most popular work relief program at that time among Members of Congress and the public. Facets of the CCC can be seen today in such youth employment and training programs as Job Corps and the Youth Conservation Corps.[42]

End Notes

[1] Based on data from the Current Employment Statistics survey, the net job loss from peak to trough of prior postwar recessions was: 2.2 million (5.0%) for the November 1948-October 1949 recession, 1.6 million (3.1%) for the July 1953-May 1954 recession, 2.1 million (4.0%) for the August 1957-April 1958 recession, 1.3 million (2.3%) for the April 1960-February 1961 recession, 0.8 million (1.2%) for the December 1969-November 1970 recession, 1.3 million (1.6%) for the November 1973-March 1975 recession, 1.0 million (1.1%) for the January 1980-July 1980 recession, 2.8 million (3.1%) for the July 1981-November 1982 recession, 1.2 million (1.1%) for the July 1990-March 1991 recession, and 1.6 million (1.2%) for the March-November 2001 recession.

[2] Based on duration of unemployment data from the Current Population Survey, previous record highs for long-term (more than 26 weeks of) unemployment were attained between November 2003 and March 2004 (24%), October 1992 (23%), June 1983 (26%), and November 1975 (21%)—after the respective ends of the March-November 2001, July 1990-March 1991, July 1981-November 1982, and November 1973-March 1975 recessions.

[3] For information on the path of the two measures following prior recessions, see CRS Report R40798, *Unemployment and Employment Trends Before and After the End of Recessions*, by Linda Levine.

[4] For a comparison of the labor market effects of the Great Depression and the latest recession, see CRS Report R40655, *The Labor Market During the Great Depression and the Current Recession*, by Linda Levine. (Hereafter cited as CRS Report R40655, *The Labor Market During the Great Depression and the Current Recession.*)

[5] From 1935-1939, it was known officially as the Works Progress Administration. From 1939 until its end in 1943, it was renamed the Works Projects Administration.

[6] William W. Bremer, "Along the "American Way": the New Deal's Work Relief Programs for the Unemployed," *Journal of American History*, vol. 62, December 1975, p. 639. (Hereafter cited as Bremer, "Along the American Way.")

[7] Job creation programs included the CCC, authorized in March 1933, making it the first work relief program operated by the federal government; the Civil Works Administration (CWA), initiated by executive order in November 1933 and operated for four months, during which time it was hoped the Public Works Administration (PWA) would be further along in starting up; and the PWA, created in Title II of the National Industrial Recovery Act, enacted in June 1933, "to stimulate industry through the purchase of materials and the payments of wages" in the construction of public works. National Resources Planning Board, *Security, Work, and Relief Policies*, Washington, DC, U.S. Government Printing Office, 1942, pp. 30-31. (Hereafter cited as National Resources Planning Board, *Security, Work, and Relief Policies.*)

[8] Bremer, "Along the American Way," p. 644. According to the National Resources Planning Board, *Security, Work, and Relief Policies,* p. 246, the CWA, PWA, and WPA could undertake such activities as highway, road, sewer, and dam construction because they were "capital improvements and services which for many years have been regarded as public, rather than private, responsibilities."

[9] National Resources Planning Board, *Security, Work, and Relief Policies*, pp. 234-238.

[10] Ibid., p. 464.

[11] In addition, Congress in Emergency Relief Appropriation Acts first excluded individuals illegally in the United States and later excluded all but U.S. citizens. Congress also established preferences for employment on WPA projects (e.g., relative need of families; veterans, the unmarried widows of veterans and wives of disabled veterans).

[12] See Table 5 in CRS Report R40655, *The Labor Market During the Great Depression and the Current Recession.*

[13] Calculated by CRS from occupational employment data of the U.S. Bureau of Labor Statistics.

[14] The ERA Act allocated the approximately $4.0 billion to finance chiefly public works activities to be undertaken by numerous federal agencies. For example, the Department of Agriculture received about $800 million, with more than half awarded to its Bureau of Public Roads, and the War Department's Corps of Engineers received about $130 million for river and harbor projects. Two emergency public employment agencies—the CCC ($600 million) and Public Works Administration ($400 million)—received funds under the act as well. Josephine Chapin Brown, *Public Relief 1929- 1939*, (NY: Octagon Books, 1971), pp. 444-446.

[15] Executive Order 7046, also issued in May 1935, required that at least 90% of program participants come from the relief rolls unless exempted by the WPA. The WPA exempted several federal agencies at their urging. Congress in large part eliminated the exemptions in the ERA Act of 1939.

[16] Federal Works Agency, *Final Report on the WPA Program, 1935-43*, (Westport, CT: Greenwood Press, 1976), p. 7. (Hereafter cited as Federal Works Agency, *Final Report on the WPA Program.*)

[17] Anthony J. Sulvetta, Norman L. Thompson, and William J. Tobin, *Alleviating Unemployment Through Accelerated Public Works in the United States: An Historical Perspective*, U.S. Department of Commerce, Economic Development Administration, Washington, DC, June 1976, pp. 14-20.

[18] Donald S. Howard, *The WPA and Federal Relief Policy,* (NY: Russell Sage Foundation, 1943). (Hereafter cited as Howard, *The WPA and Federal Relief Policy.*)

[19] Arthur W. MacMahon, John D. Millett, and Gladys Ogden, *The Administration of Federal Work Relief*, (NY, Da Capo Press, 1971), p. 126.

[20] Federal Works Agency, *Final Report of the WPA Program*, pp. 28-3 0.

[21] National Resources Planning Board, *Security, Work, and Relief Policies*, p. 236.

[22] Federal Works Agency, *Final Report of the WPA Program*, pp. 47-54.

[23] Ibid., pp. 59-70.

[24] Howard, *The WPA and Federal Relief Policy*, p. 144.

[25] Ibid., p. 150.

[26] Ibid., pp. 486-492.

[27] Federal Works Agency, *Final Report on the WPA Program*, p. 22.

[28] Ibid., p. 24.

[29] John A. Salmond, *The Civilian Conservation Corps, 1933-1942: A New Deal Case Study*, (Durham, NC: Duke University Press, 1967), p. 12. (Hereafter cited as Salmond, *The Civilian Conservation Corps.*)

[30] Each enrollee—regardless of where they came from or a camp's location—received a monthly cash allowance of $30. Most of it was given to their families.

[31] The number of enrollees peaked at more than 500,000 in 1935. For comparison purposes, there were perhaps 2 million unemployed men between the ages of 14 and 24 in 1940. See Table 4 in CRS Report R40655, *The Labor Market During the Great Depression and the Current Recession*, which also discusses the paucity of labor force data available before 1948.

[32] An education program had been established after much internal wrangling in late 1933. Salmond, *The Civilian Conservation Corps*, pp. 47-54. For information on the education program from 1937 until the CCC's end in 1943, see Salmond, *The Civilian Conservation Corps*, pp. 162-168.

[33] National Resources Planning Board, *Security, Work, and Relief Policies*, pp. 261, 264.

[34] Ibid., pp. 67-68.

[35] Over the course of its existence, it sometimes was required that youth enrollees be from families on relief.

[36] Salmond, *The Civilian Conservation Corps*, p. 27.

[37] National Resources Planning Board, *Security, Work, and Relief Policies*, pp. 67-68, 261.

[38] Ibid., pp. 261-262.

[39] Salmond, *The Civilian Conservation Corps*, pp. 12 1-126.

[40] Ibid., pp. 128-132.

[41] Economic value might be measured as the cost of outcomes (e.g., road construction) had they been undertaken by the private sector.

[42] CRS Report RL33975, *Vulnerable Youth: Background and Policies*, by Adrienne L. Fernandes.

In: Recession, Depression, and Unemployment ISBN: 978-1-61761-508-5
Editors: Daniel A. García

Chapter 7

U.S. ECONOMY IN RECESSION: SIMILARITIES TO AND DIFFERENCES FROM THE PAST

Marc Labonte

SUMMARY

According to the National Bureau of Economic Research (NBER), the U.S. economy entered a recession in December 2007. It is now the longest recession of the post-World War II era. The recession can be separated into two distinct phases. During the first phase, which lasted for the first half of 2008, the recession was not deep as measured by the decline in gross domestic product (GDP) or the rise in unemployment. It then deepened from the third quarter of 2008 to the first quarter of 2009. The economy continued to contract slightly in the second quarter of 2009, before beginning to grow in the third quarter. This recession features the largest decline in output, consumption, and investment, and the largest increase in unemployment, of any post-war recession.

Previously, the longest and deepest of the post-war recessions were those beginning in 1973 and 1981. Both of those recessions took place in a context of high inflation that made the Federal Reserve (Fed) hesitant to aggressively reduce interest rates to stimulate economic activity. The Fed has not shown a similar reluctance in the current recession, bringing short-term rates down to zero. Although inflation exceeded the Fed's "comfort zone" in 2007 and 2008, it was not nearly as high as it was in the 1970s or 1980s recessions, and it began decelerating in the second half of 2008. Economists are divided over whether inflation or deflation (falling prices) is a bigger threat going forward.

Both the 1973 and 1981 recessions also featured large spikes in oil prices near the beginning of the recession—as did the current one. Oil markets' disruptions and recessions have gone hand in hand throughout the post-war period.

The previous two recessions (beginning in 1991 and 2001) were unusually mild and brief, but subsequently featured long "jobless recoveries" where growth was sluggish and unemployment continued to rise. Since this recession has been neither brief nor mild (since the third quarter of 2008), it is unclear whether another jobless recovery should be expected.

A decline in residential investment (house building) during a recession is not unusual, and it is not uncommon for residential investment to decline more sharply than business investment and to begin declining before the recession. The current contraction in residential investment is unusually severe, however, as indicated by the atypical decline in national house prices.

One unique characteristic of the current recession is the severe disruption to financial markets. Financial conditions began to deteriorate in August 2007, but became more severe in September 2008. While financial downturns commonly accompany economic downturns, financial markets have continued to function smoothly in previous recessions. This difference has led some commentators to instead compare the current recession to the Great Depression. While the onset of both crises bear some similarities, to date, the effects on the broader economy have little in common. In the first year of the Great Depression, GDP fell by almost 9%, prices fell by 2.5%, and unemployment rose from 3.2% to 8.7% (eventually peaking at 24.9%). The change in GDP, prices, and unemployment in the current recession to date has not been significantly different from other deeper post-war recessions. Most economists blame the severity of the Great Depression on policy errors—notably, the decision to allow the money supply to contract and thousands of banks to fail. By contrast, policymakers have aggressively intervened to ease monetary policy and provide direct assistance to the financial sector in the current recession.

INTRODUCTION

The U.S. economy officially entered a recession in December 2007. To determine what type of policy intervention, if any, might be needed to mitigate the recession, Congress is concerned with how long and deep the recession would be without additional intervention. This chapter provides information on the patterns found across past recessions since World War II and analyzes whether and how this recession might be different.

There is no simple rule-of-thumb to determine when recessions begin or end. Recessions are officially declared by the National Bureau of Economic Research (NBER), a non-profit research organization.[1] The NBER defines a recession as a "significant decline in economic activity spread across the economy, lasting more than a few months" based on a number of economic indicators, with an emphasis on trends in employment and income.[2] It is unlikely that all of those indicators will begin declining or rising simultaneously. Thus, when comparing historical episodes, some of the symptoms associated with a recession may occur before or after the recession has officially begun or ended. In the current episode, gross domestic product (GDP) began to fall (in the fourth quarter of 2007) before employment (in January 2008), and both deteriorated significantly in the third quarter of 2008. The economy began to grow again in the third quarter of 2009, but employment has continued to fall.

The NBER does not declare the beginning or end of the recession until after the fact. Thus, the length of the recession will not be known until after the fact. At some point in the future, the NBER may decide that the recession has already ended.

THE LENGTH AND DEPTH OF RECESSIONS

Recessions are not uncommon—2008 marked the 11th since World War II. In recent years, recessions have been less frequent—from 1982 to 2001, there were only two recessions—but the length between the current one and the prior one, 73 months, was comparable to the frequency of recessions from 1945 to 1981.

As can be seen from Table 1, the current recession is the longest of the post-war period.[3]The median length of post-war recessions is 9.5 months. Recessions end because of monetary and fiscal stimulus—both have already been employed in the current episode[4]—and because markets automatically adjust. Although unique circumstances caused the current recession, the unusual length of the recession to date and the return to economic growth in the third quarter suggests that the recession may be coming to an end. Forecasters predict that the economy will continue to grow in the next few quarters.[5]

Recessions affect economic well-being by their length and depth. When considering depth, the current recession can be separated into two distinct phases. During the first phase, which lasted for the first two quarters of 2008, the recession was not deep as measured by the gross domestic product (GDP) or unemployment. It deepened in the third quarter of 2008, however, and remained deep through the first quarter of 2009. After a slight further decline in the second quarter, the economy began to grow again in the third quarter of 2009.

Table 1. Economic Indicators During Post-War Recessions

Dates	Duration (months)	Cumulative Percent Change		
		GDP	Consumption	Investment
Nov. 1948 - Oct. 1949	11	-1.6%	3.4%	-10.2%
July 1953 - May 1954	10	-2.6	-0.5	-3.4
Aug. 1957 - April 1958	8	-3.7	-1.3	-8.0
April 1960 - Feb. 1961	10	-1.6	1.0	-5.1
Dec. 1969 - Nov. 1970	11	-0.6	2.5	-2.6
Nov. 1973 - March 1975	16	-2.8	-0.7	-18.4
Jan. 1980 - July 1980	6	-2.2	-1.2	-8.1
July 1981 - Nov. 1982	16	-2.7	0.1	-9.3
July 1990 - Mar. 1991	8	-1.4	-0.7	-7.2
March 2001 - Nov. 2001	8	0	1.2	-3.2
Dec. 2007 – n/a	n/a	-3.7[a]	- 1 .9[a]	-21 .0[a]

Source: National Bureau of Economic Research; CRS calculations based on data from Bureau of Labor Statistics, Bureau of Economic Analysis.

Notes: Table measures changes in economic indicators from peak to trough, which do not always correspond with NBER business cycle dates. Investment growth excludes changes in inventories.

a. End of current recession has not yet been announced. Data measured from GDP peak in 2007:4 to GDP trough in 2009:2.

Through the second quarter of 2009, the fall in GDP during the current recession, a cumulative 3.7%, matched the recession beginning in 1957 as the deepest of the post-war period. The decline in output after the second quarter of 2008 was even larger. Most of the decline occurred from the third quarter of 2008 to the first quarter of 2009. The 1981 recession was the last recession to feature consecutive quarters of steep declines in GDP.

Table 2. The Unemployment Rate at a Recession's End and at the Rate's Peak

Dates of Business Cycle Peak and Trough	Unemployment Rate at Expansion Peak	Unemployment Rate at Recession Trough	Peak Unemployment Rate	
			Level	Date
Nov. 1948 - Oct. 1949	3.8%	7.9%	7.9%	Oct. 1949
July 1953 - May 1954	2.6%	5.9%	6.1%	Sept. 1954
Aug. 1957 - Apr. 1958	4.1%	7.4%	7.5%	July 1958
Apr. 1960 - Feb. 1961	5.2%	6.9%	7.1%	May 1961
Dec. 1969 - Nov. 1970	3.5%	5.9%	6.1%	Aug. 1971
Nov. 1973 - Mar. 1975	4.8%	8.6%	9.0%	May 1975
Jan. 1980 - July 1980	6.3%	7.8%	7.8%	July 1980
July 1981 - Nov. 1982	7.2%	10.8%	10.8%	Nov. 1982
July 1990 - Mar. 1991	5.5%	6.8%	7.8%	June 1992
Mar. 2001 - Nov. 2001	4.3%	5.5%	6.3%	July 2003

Source: CRS Report R40798, *Unemployment and Employment Trends Before and After the End of Recessions*, based on data from the Bureau of Labor Statistics.

The 1973 and 1981 recessions were also unusually long and deep, in terms of lost output. During the recession beginning in 1973, gross domestic product (GDP) fell by a cumulative 3%. During the recession beginning in 1981, GDP fell by a cumulative 2.9%, and this recession came on the heels of a 2.2% decline in GDP in a separate recession one year earlier.

Economists often attribute the unusual length and depth of the 1973 and 1981 recessions in part to the Federal Reserve's decision to keep interest rates high. The federal funds rate peaked at 12.9% in July 1974 and 19% in July 1981. (After adjusting for inflation, these rates were not nearly as high as they appear because inflation was so much higher at the time.) The Fed had raised rates that high in order to reduce inflation, which, as measured in the GDP accounts, peaked at an annualized rate of 12.8% in the third quarter of 1974 and 11.1% in the fourth quarter of 1980. For that reason, some economists have described these recessions as "made in Washington"—had the Fed not raised rates so high, they argue, the recessions would presumably have been shorter and milder (although inflationary problems might have worsened).

This dynamic has not been important in the current recession, as the federal funds rate's recent peak was 5.25%. Rising inflation was initially a concern in the current episode, but has never come close to the rates of the 1970s and 1980s—it peaked at 4.2% in the first quarter of 2007. Rising energy and commodity prices were temporarily pushing inflation up in the first half of 2008; since then, declines in those prices have temporarily pushed inflation to very low rates. Going forward, views are divided on the outlook for inflation. Some commentators point to a federal funds rate of zero and the unprecedented scale of the Fed's intervention in financial markets as policies that will ultimately push inflation higher. Through direct lending and asset purchases, the Fed's outstanding support to the financial sector has, at times, exceeded $1 trillion, compared to less than $1 billion before the financial crisis began.[6] In normal times, such interest rate and lending policies would be expected to be highly inflationary. But as the recession drives down aggregate demand, it puts downward pressure on inflation. Other commentators fear that the recession will be severe enough that avoiding deflation (falling prices) should be a greater priority than inflation. They argue that the Fed's intervention in financial markets is necessary to avoid a "liquidity trap," where lower interest rates no longer stimulate interest-sensitive spending. Although the Fed has brought the federal funds rate down to near zero, since it was only 5.25% when the Fed began reducing rates, the Fed's scope for easing monetary policy through traditional methods was somewhat limited. By contrast, the federal funds rate, although high, was reduced (peak to trough) by 6.8 percentage points in the 1973 recession and by 10.5 percentage points in the 1981 recession.

UNEMPLOYMENT IN RECESSIONS

Table 2 shows the rise in unemployment in previous post-war recessions. Unsurprisingly, the recessions with the deepest decline in output also featured the largest increases in unemployment. From low to post-recession high, the 1973 recession saw an increase in the unemployment rate of 4.4 percentage points, and the 1981 recession saw an increase of 3.6 percentage points (or 4.8 percentage points compared to the expansion that ended in 1980). As of October 2009, the unemployment rate has risen 5.3 percentage points, and many forecasters are predicting that unemployment will continue to rise until 2010.[7]

Most of the increase in unemployment in the current recession occurred after the first six months of the recession, underlining the initial mildness of the recession. The rise in the unemployment rate during this recession was comparable to the recessions since 1960 for the first 10 months following the recession's onset. Beginning in the 11th month, however, it followed a pattern similar but even more severe than the two "deep and long" recessions of 1973 and 1980. (Unemployment leveled off after about a year in the other four recessions since 1960.) The current recession eventually featured the largest increase in unemployment in the post-war period. Unemployment has been rising for 22 months and counting, as of October 2009. The 1973 and 1981 recession were the only other two in the post-war period where unemployment continued to rise after about a year; in the 1973 recession, it rose for 19 months.

The previous two recessions, in 1991 and 2001, were mild and brief as measured by the decline in GDP. Further, the increases in unemployment during both recessions were among the smallest in the post-war period. This is not the whole story, however, because, in both cases, unemployment continued to rise for over a year after the recession had ended. (In every other post-war recession, with the exception of the one beginning in November 1970, unemployment began falling within six months of the recession's end.) These two episodes have been called "jobless recoveries." If the rise in unemployment in the jobless recovery were included, the episode beginning in 1991 would have featured an above average rise in unemployment; but the episode beginning in 2001 would still remain below average. It is unclear whether the economy has changed in some fundamental way that makes jobless recoveries likely from now on, or if it was simply a coincidence that the last two recessions ended in this way. Since this recession has been neither brief nor mild, another jobless recovery should not necessarily be expected. All of the recessions followed by jobless recoveries featured a mild decline in GDP growth during the recession and weak GDP growth during the jobless recovery period. So whether there is a jobless recovery following the current recession is likely to depend on how strong economic growth is in the initial recovery period. The deep decline in output since the fourth quarter of 2008 makes rapid growth possible but not inevitable. One potential barrier to rapid growth would be continuing disruption in financial markets (see "Recessions and the Financial Sector" below).

Consumption and Investment in Recessions

The current recession has also featured the largest decrease in consumption and private fixed investment spending. There are a few commonalities found across all previous post-war recessions. First, in all cases, consumption spending did not weaken as much as GDP, as shown in Table 1. In fact, in five out of 10 recessions, consumption continued to grow while GDP fell. To the extent that households can adjust their saving and borrowing levels, they are thought to generally prefer to "smooth" consumption over time, avoiding sudden increases and decreases. In the current recession, consumption declined relatively rapidly in the third and fourth quarters of 2008, with small positive and negative changes in the other quarters. Consistent with the historical pattern, consumption has fallen by proportionately less than output cumulatively for the recession so far.

Second, in all recessions, fixed investment spending fell more sharply than GDP. This evidence casts doubt on the popular explanation that recessions are caused by declines in consumption. It suggests that the primary driver of the business cycle is cyclical changes in investment demand. Investment demand can be separated into two categories—business investment (in plant and equipment) and residential investment (home building). Cyclical changes in business investment could be driven by changes in business conditions, confidence, or credit conditions. Residential investment is driven by changes in housing demand and credit conditions. Changes in credit conditions are heavily influenced by monetary policy.

Both business investment and residential investment fell in each of the post-war recessions. In eight out of 10 recessions, there was a larger percentage decline in residential investment than in business investment.[8] To date, the percentage decline in residential investment has been much larger in the current recession—business investment did not begin to fall until the third quarter of 2008. (Since then, it has fallen sharply.) Further, in nine out of 10 past recessions, the decline in residential investment preceded the decline in GDP growth.[9] This pattern held in the current recession as well. Many economists have argued that the housing crash was the root cause of the current recession. The fact that the decline in residential investment preceded the decline in GDP is not necessarily evidence that housing crashes have also caused other post-war recessions. It may be that recessions are caused by a tightening in credit conditions, and residential investment is the sector that is first and most affected by tighter credit conditions. For example, the deep decline in residential investment in the early 1980s is usually attributed to the Fed's decision to push the federal funds rate as high as 19%. While residential investment has fallen in all other post-war recessions, national house prices have not since the major data series were first collected, until now.[10] National house prices fell 12% peak to trough,[11] and residential investment fell by about half from peak to trough. These data indicate that the current housing crash has been more severe than others. Unlike many other post-war recessions, housing may be a cause, rather than a symptom, of the current recession.

Recessions and OilPrices

Another commonality between this recession and past recessions is the behavior of oil prices. The recessions of 1973 and the early 1980s are remembered for their oil shocks, and this pattern is not uncommon. In a famous article, economist James Hamilton identified disruptions to oil supply before all but one of the post-war recessions—a pattern that has continued in every recession since his article was published, including the latest. [12] Crude oil prices rose from $51 per barrel in January 2007 to a peak of $129 per barrel in July 2008. By the end of 2008, prices had fallen by half, which should eventually offset much of the contractionary effects of the previous price increase on GDP. Evidence against attributing the economic downturn to rising oil prices would be the fact that oil prices rose significantly in the previous expansion without any noticeable effect on GDP growth. For example, prices rose from $37 per barrel in December 2004 to $69 per barrel in July 2006.

Recessions and the World Economy

As a result of the current global nature of the financial turmoil, economists are projecting that there will be a global recession as well.[13] In 2009, the

International Monetary Fund (IMF) projects that world GDP growth will be -3.4% in developed economies, contracting in all of the G-7 economies,[14] and -1.1% in the world overall.[15] A widespread recession would not be unusual. For example, between 1980 and 1982, all of the G-7 countries except France and Japan experienced a contraction in GDP for at least one year (and growth was close to zero in France in 1981). Likewise, between 1991 and 1993, all of the G-7 countries except Japan experienced a contraction in GDP for at least one year (and growth was close to zero in Japan in 1992 and 1993). The global nature of the recession could potentially prolong and deepen it because there would be less demand abroad for a country's exports. In a study of historical recessions in industrial countries, the IMF found that recessions that were highly synchronized internationally lasted an average of four months longer and GDP fell an average of 1% more than other recessions.[16]

Recessions and the Financial Sector

As noted above, the data available indicate an initially mild recession that historical patterns suggest might not persist much longer. Evidence in favor of predicting a longer and deeper recession is the severity of the financial downturn that began in August 2007 and worsened in September 2008. In the fourth quarter, the decline in GDP accelerated markedly. While a diminished investor appetite for risk and a stock market decline before or during a recession is common, this recession has featured a breakdown in activity in certain financial markets, such as the markets for asset backed securities, commercial paper, and interbank lending, and the failure (or government rescue to avoid failure) of several large, established financial firms. Since then, financial conditions have improved but have not returned to normal. Beginning in the fourth quarter of 2008, disruptions in financial markets resulted in significant declines in business investment. Given the lag between changes in financial conditions and economic activity, it is plausible that the recession could continue through 2009, even though the historical pattern would suggest that, after over a year and a half, a recovery would not be far off. In a study of historical recessions in industrial countries, the IMF found that recessions associated with financial crises lasted an average of seven months longer, although the change in GDP was not statistically significant from other recessions.[17]

COMPARISONSBETWEEN THE CURRENTRECESSION AND THE GREAT DEPRESSION

Some commentators have suggested that the financial crisis makes the Great Depression a more relevant comparison than the other post-war recessions to present-day conditions. While the current financial downturn has been the most severe in the post-war period by many measures, there are many differences between the current situation and the Great Depression. While the stock market crash of 1929 played a role in setting the economic downturn in motion, there is a consensus among economists that policy errors caused the downturn to become the Great Depression.[18] Among the most important errors were the Fed's failure to counteract the contraction in the money supply, which caused overall prices to fall a cumulative 25%, and bank runs which caused thousands of banks to fail. (The money supply fell primarily in order to maintain the gold standard, and the economic growth rate was high after the United States left the gold standard.)

By contrast, policymakers have responded aggressively and unconventionally to attempt to contain the current crisis. The Federal Reserve (Fed) has reduced short-term interest rates to nearly zero. Direct Fed assistance outstanding to the financial system has exceeded $1 trillion, and Congress has authorized Treasury to provide an additional $700 billion to the financial system through the Troubled Assets Relief Program. [19] Widespread bank runs have not occurred since the introduction of deposit insurance in the 1930s, and similar runs on money market mutual funds in 2008 were circumvented when Treasury temporarily guaranteed their principal. The Federal Deposit Insurance Corporation (FDIC) also temporarily guaranteed certain bank debt to ensure that banks would not lose access to borrowing markets.

During the Great Depression, policymakers were also reluctant to stimulate the economy through fiscal expansion (a larger structural budget deficit).[20] By contrast, the budget deficit increased as a share of GDP from 1.2% in 2007 to 10% in 2009. There was also a belief among some policymakers at the time that recessions were healthy processes that purged the economy of inefficiently allocated resources—a view that fell out of favor as the Depression worsened, and was eventually replaced by the view that prudent policy changes could avoid the needless waste of resources laid idle by recessions.

The Great Depression included two recessions, with the first lasting 3½ years and the second, beginning four years later, lasting another year. The current recession started too recently to compare it to the entire period, but a comparison of data now and during the first year of the recession indicate that the current recession so far has much more in common with other post-war recessions than with the Great Depression. In the first year of the Great Depression, GDP fell almost 9%, prices fell 2.5%, and unemployment rose from 3.2% to 8.7% (eventually peaking at 24.9%). By contrast, GDP rose 0.4% for 2008 overall, prices rose almost 4%, and the unemployment rate rose from 4.6% to 5.8%.[21]

End Notes

[1] The NBER announced in December 2008 that the current recession began in December 2007. For more information, see CRS Report R40052, *What is a Recession and Who Decided When It Started?*, by Brian W. Cashell.

[2] National Bureau of Economic Research, *Determination of the December 2007 Peak in Economic Activity*, January 7, 2008, http://www.nber.org/cycles

[3] Another possibility is that the NBER could have dated the beginning of the recession later in 2008, once unemployment began rising more quickly. If it had, then the recession to date would have been shorter, and perhaps further from its conclusion.

[4] For a review of policy steps already taken and current policy proposals, see CRS Report R40 104, *Economic Stimulus: Issues and Policies*, by Jane G. Gravelle, Thomas L. Hungerford, and Marc Labonte.

[5] See, for example, *Blue Chip Economic Indicators*, vol. 34, no. 10, October 10, 2009.

[6] See CRS Report RL34427, *Financial Turmoil: Federal Reserve Policy Responses*, by Marc Labonte.

[7] See, for example, *Blue Chip Economic Indicators*, vol. 34, no. 10, October 10, 2009.

[8] Since business investment accounts for a larger share of GDP than residential investment, the decline in dollar terms was not always larger.

[9] Economist Edward Leamer estimates that residential investment is responsible for 26% of the weakening in the economy before the average recession, and 11% of the weakness during the recession. Edward Leamer, "Housing is the Business Cycle," *National Bureau of Economic Research working paper*, no. 13428 (September 2007).

[10] Prices may have fallen during the Great Depression and previous recessions for which official data are not available.

[11] Based on the Federal Housing Finance Administration's Purchase-Only House Price Index, a national measure of single-family houses with conforming mortgages based on resale data.

[12] James Hamilton, "Oil and the Macroeconomy Since World War II," Journal of Political Economy, vol. 91, no. 2, 1983, p. 228.

[13] See CRS Report RL34742, *The Global Financial Crisis: Analysis and Policy Implications*, coordinated by Dick K. Nanto.

[14] The G-7 countries consist of the United States, United Kingdom, France, Italy, Germany, Canada, and Japan.

[15] International Monetary Fund, *World Economic Outlook*, Washington, DC, October 2009.

[16] International Monetary Fund, *World Economic Outlook*, Washington, DC, April 2009, p. 111.

[17] International Monetary Fund, *World Economic Outlook*, Washington, DC, April 2009, p. 111. See also Carmen Reinhart and Kenneth Rogoff, "The Aftermath of Financial Crises," *National Bureau of Economic Research*, working paper no. 14656 (January 2009).

[18] For an overview, see Ben Bernanke, "The Macroeconomics of the Great Depression: A Comparative Approach," *Journal of Money, Credit, and Banking*, vol. 27, no. 1 (February 1995).

[19] See CRS Report RL34730, *Troubled Asset Relief Program: Legislation and Treasury Implementation*, by Baird Webel and Edward V. Murphy.

[20] Much of the increase in the budget deficit during the Great Depression was caused by falling revenues due to the Depression, rather than the introduction of new policy measures that were deficit-financed. The structural budget deficit refers to the budget deficit that would occur in the absence of changes in economic conditions.

[21] Quarterly data does not exist for the 1920s and 193 0s, so this comparison is for annual data in 1930 and 2008. Percent changes for annual data compare the mid-point of the current year to the mid-point of the previous year.

In: Recession, Depression, and Unemployment ISBN: 978-1-61761-508-5
Editors: Daniel A. García

Chapter 8

WHAT IS A RECESSION AND WHO DECIDED WHEN IT STARTED?

Brian W. Cashell

SUMMARY

The National Bureau of Economic Research (NBER) recently announced that the economy had reached a cyclical peak and that a recession had begun in December 2007. A recession is one of several discrete phases in the overall business cycle. The term may often be used loosely to describe an economy that is slowing down or characterized by weakness in at least one major sector like the housing market. When used by economists, "recession" means a significant decline in overall economic activity that lasts more than a few months. NBER business cycle dating committee is the generally recognized arbiter of the dates of the beginnings and ends of recessions. With all statistics it takes some time to compile the data, which means they are only available after the events they describe. Moreover, because it takes time to discern changes in trends given the usual month-to-month volatility in economic indicators, and because the data are subject to revision, it takes some time before the dating committee can agree that a recession began at a certain date. It can be a year or more after the fact that the dating committee announces the date of the beginning of a recession. Just as it took some time for the business cycle dating committee to determine when the recession began, it is likely to be some time after the fact that they determine when the recession has come to an end.

Introduction

On December 1, 2008, the National Bureau of Economic Research confirmed what many had suspected for some time – that the economy was in a recession. They announced that the economy had reached a cyclical peak, and that a recession had begun in December 2007. The term "recession" may often be used loosely to describe an economy that is slowing down or characterized by weakness in at least one major sector like the housing market. When economists use the term, however, they try to do so consistently. Recessions typically have common characteristics and so economists try to identify the beginning and ending dates of recessions in order to further their overall understanding of the economy.

Whatis a Recession?

A recession is one of several discrete phases in the overall business cycle. The beginning of a recession is known as a business cycle "peak," and the end of a recession is referred to as a business cycle "trough." In 1946, Arthur Burns and Wesley Mitchell published a study of business cycles and offered a definition intended as a guide for further study:

> Business cycles are a type of fluctuation found in the aggregate economic activity of nations that organize their work mainly in business enterprises: a cycle consists of expansions occurring at about the same time in many economic activities, followed by similarly general recessions, contractions, and revivals which merge into the expansion phase of the next cycle.[1]

This definition requires both expansions and recessions to be apparent in *many economic activities* at about the same time, which would seem to exclude an economy exhibiting weakness in a single market.

More recently, economists at the National Bureau of Economic Research (NBER), issued a memo with a slightly more precise definition:

> A recession is a significant decline in economic activity spread across the economy, lasting more than a few months, normally visible in real GDP, real income, employment, industrial production, and wholesale-retail sales. A recession begins just after the economy reaches a peak of activity and ends as the economy reaches its trough. Between trough and peak, the economy is in an expansion. Expansion is the normal state of the economy; most recessions are brief and they have been rare in recent decades.[2]

This is the generally accepted view among economists of what constitutes an economic recession. There is also a commonly cited "rule of thumb" that is referred to in the press. That rule is that a recession is two consecutive quarterly declines in real gross domestic product (GDP). But this rule does not always apply. For example, there was a recession beginning in March 2001 and ending in November 2001 that was not characterized by two successive quarterly declines in real GDP.

In any case, an important distinction is that a recession is a period of declining output and not just a period of slower economic growth. It is possible for GDP growth to be positive yet so slow that the unemployment rate rises. This is sometimes referred to as a "growth recession."

WHO DECIDES WHEN THE U.S. ECONOMY IS IN A RECESSION?

Among economists, the NBER is the generally accepted arbiter of business cycle turning points.[3] The NBER is a private nonprofit and nonpartisan organization that was founded in 1920. In the beginning its focus was on the macroeconomy, business cycles, and long-term growth, but now it seeks to promote research on a wide variety of topics. For many years, the NBER itself determined the dates of swings in the business cycle. In 1978, however, a separate *business cycle dating committee* was formed. The members of the committee are appointed by the president of the NBER, and they are now responsible for determining the dates of the beginnings and ends of recessions.[4] The current members of this committee are

- Robert Hall, Chair – Director of NBER's Program of Research on Economic Fluctuations and Growth, and Professor at Stanford University;

- Martin Feldstein – President Emeritus of NBER, and Professor at Harvard University;
- Jeffrey Frankel – Director of NBER's Program in International Finance and Macroeconomics, and Professor at Harvard University;
- Robert J. Gordon – NBER Research Associate, and Professor at Northwestern University;
- James Poterba – NBER President, and Professor at MIT;
- David Romer – Professor at the University of California, Berkeley;
- Victor Zarnowitz – Senior Fellow at the Conference Board, and Professor Emeritus at the University of Chicago.

HOW DO WE KNOW WHEN A RECESSIONSTARTS?

One important indicator of economic conditions is growth in real gross domestic product (GDP). GDP statistics are compiled each quarter, and thus there is a time lag between the first month that is reflected in the data and the release of the data. For example, the first release of data for the first calendar quarter of a given year does not occur until late April. The data from that release is subject to revision in each of the next two months and may be revised later on as well. It is not inconceivable that a first release of data that showed a decline in real GDP would later be revised to show an increase. Even so, those using the rule of thumb that two successive quarterly declines in real GDP constitutes a recession would have to wait for the release of the second quarter data in August to establish that a recession began at the start of the year.

Because of the time lag associated with the release of GDP data, and because business cycle turning points are associated with months rather than quarters, the dating committee relies on a number of monthly economic indicators. Among the more important monthly indicators the committee looks at are personal income, employment, and industrial production. Even in the case of monthly indicators, it may require several months of data to establish a change in trends.

When there is a recession, not all of the economic indicators may show a change in trend at the same time. Historically, some indicators, such as housing starts and the stock market, tend to slow or decline in advance of a recession, and some, like the unemployment rate tend to react to changing conditions with a lag.

Table 1. Dates of Recent Business Cycle Turning Points and the Dates They Were Announced by the NBER

Turning Point	Date of Turning Point	Date Turning Point was announced by NBER	Months After Turning Point
peak	January 1980	June 3, 1980	5
trough	July 1980	July 8, 1981	12
peak	July 1981	January 6, 1982	6
trough	November 1982	July 8, 1983	8
peak	July 1990	April 25, 1991	9
trough	March 1991	December 22, 1992	21
peak	March 2001	November 26, 2001	8
trough	November 2001	July 17, 2003	20
peak	December 2007	December 1, 2008	12

Source: National Bureau of Economic Research.

With all statistics it takes some time to compile the data, which means that the statistics are only available after the events they describe. Moreover, because it takes time to discern changes in trends given the usual month-to-month volatility in economic indicators, and because the data are subject to revision, it takes some time before the dating committee can agree that a recession (or an expansion) began at a certain date. Table 1 shows, for recent business cycle peaks and troughs, the date of the turning point and the date when the committee issued a release identifying the date of the turning point.

The longest delay between the beginning of a new phase of the business cycle and its announcement was when a recession was found to have ended in March 1991 but was not announced until 21 months had passed. The shortest delay was five months after the expansion ended in January 1980. Of the eight examples shown here, four were not announced until at least a year had elapsed.

RHETORICAL AND ANALYTICALSIGNIFICANCE

While all recessions have unique characteristics, they also have many common aspects. Thus they are the object of economic analysis both individually and collectively. Because they are undesirable, economists study them in the hope that they can advise policymakers how to avoid them. To do so, it is important to agree on a chronology, and it may not be an inconvenience to economists that it takes time to establish one.

Policymakers, on the other hand, are more concerned with the present and the immediate future. If they hope to avert or mitigate the consequences of recession, they cannot wait for an "official" declaration. By then the recession may be history.

Although there can be a significant delay between the onset of a recession and the dating committee determination, there is often little doubt that the economy is, or has been, in recession well before the announcement.[5] For policy measures to have mitigating effects, they must be timely. Policymakers may not have the luxury of holding themselves to as strict a definition of recession as economic analysts.

End Notes

[1] Arthur F. Burns and Wesley C. Mitchell, Measuring Business Cycles, National Bureau of Economic Research, 1946, p. 3.

[2] Business Cycle Dating Committee, Memo, National Bureau of Economic Research, Jan. 7, 2008, 3 pp. Available on the internet at http://www.nber.org/cycles

[3] The NBER website is at http://www.nber.org.

[4] A working paper published by the Bureau of Economic Analysis found that "[t]he NBER dating committee's methodology appears to be very robust." See Bruce T. Grimm, "Alternative Measures of U.S. Economic Activity in Business Cycles and Business Cycle Dating," Bureau of Economic Analysis Working Paper 2005-05, Aug. 2005.

[5] Just as it took some time for the business cycle dating committee to determine when the recession began, it is likely to be some time after the fact that they determine when the recession has come to an end.

In: Recession, Depression, and Unemployment ISBN: 978-1-61761-508-5
Editors: Daniel A. García

Chapter 9

LOSING A JOB DURING A RECESSION

United States Congressional Budget Office

Each year, even when the economy is growing, millions of people lose a job for reasons other than poor performance or misconduct. The ability of employers to quickly adjust the size of their workforces in response to changes in demand is generally considered a source of strength for the U.S. economy over the long term, because it prompts a shift of labor resources toward areas of higher productivity. Some people, however, bear substantial costs from employers' flexibility—particularly during recessions, when many people lose jobs and new opportunities are relatively scarce.

This issue brief reviews the research on the short- and long-term effects of involuntary job loss for reasons other than poor performance or misconduct on people's future employment and earnings.[1] In light of the recession that began in December 2007 and the Congressional Budget Office's (CBO's) projection that, under current law, the unemployment rate will remain elevated for a number of years, the brief focuses on the effects of involuntary job loss during periods of weak economic activity.[2] The brief also summarizes some of the government programs that help people who have lost their job.

Many people who lose a job involuntarily find a new job, some quite quickly (within a month or so) and others after more time. Loss of a job often means a loss of health insurance for the worker and perhaps for his or her family, though the recently enacted health care legislation will enhance the opportunities for people to purchase health insurance. Some people who lose a job involuntarily do not find a new job. Some of those people may decide not to look for a new job, while others may look for a job but be unsuccessful in their search. Even among workers who find a new job, many end up with lower earnings, not only in the short term but also over a period of many years.

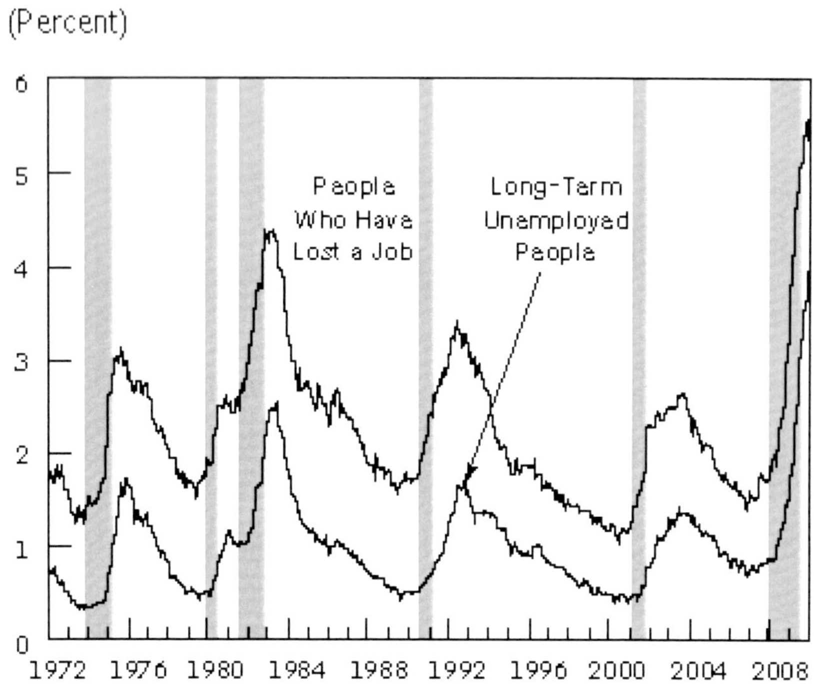

Source: Congressional Budget Office based on data from the Bureau of Labor Statistics (BLS).

Notes: The percentage of people who have lost a job comes from the data series titled "Lost Job, BLS Definition." That series includes unemployed people who involuntarily lost their last job, including people fired for poor performance, and those who completed a temporary job. It only includes people available and looking for work and excludes people on temporary layoff.

Long-term unemployed people are those who have been unemployed for at least 27 consecutive weeks.

The shaded vertical bars indicate the duration of recessions. The National Bureau of Economic Research establishes the dates on which recessions begin and end but has not yet done so for the end of the most recent recession, which is shown as having ended in the second quarter of 2009.

Figure 1. Selected Categories of Unemployed People, as a Percentage of the Labor Force.

Several points warrant attention at the outset. First, outcomes for people who lose their job "for cause"—that is, because of their poor performance on the job—may differ significantly from those examined in this brief. Second, the best information on the consequences of job loss during recessions necessarily comes from past recessions, because data regarding job loss during the most recent recession are generally not yet available. But no two recessions are alike: The most recent recession is associated with a specific set of challenging circumstances, so the labor market downturn has been especially severe, and output is expected to grow fairly slowly during this recovery.[3] Third, many of the results presented in this brief represent what might be expected to happen, on average, to people who lose a job during a recession. The array of actual outcomes is quite broad, however. Some people who lose a job during a recession will recover quickly, while others will suffer worse effects than the average person who lost a job. Fourth, job loss has many potential consequences that are not discussed here. For example, people who lose a job tend to have more health problems later in life, their family life can suffer, and entire communities may struggle, especially if job loss is concentrated in particular geographic areas.[4]

EMPLOYMENTAFTERINVOLUNTARY JOB LOSS

Involuntary job loss generally results from the operating decisions of an employer. It can happen with varying amounts of advance notice, ranging from a sudden and unexpected shutdown to layoffs or plant closings announced several months in advance. In either case, many people attempt to find a new job that is similar to their last one, while others may change careers or pursue interests outside of the paid workforce. Finding a new job is usually more difficult when the economy is weak.

Finding a New Job

Some people who lose their job in an unfavorable labor market find work relatively quickly, but others take a long time. Among people who were displaced from their job in 2003—when the unemployment rate peaked at 6 percent—and were reemployed by January 2006, CBO found that 10 percent were reemployed within a week.[5] Another 25 percent found a job within a month. In contrast, 25 percent were jobless (although not necessarily searching for work) for six months or more. In 2009, the fraction of the labor force consisting of unemployed people who lost their last job (including those who were fired for poor performance) and the fraction that had been unemployed for 27 weeks or more (the so-called longterm unemployed) were well above their previous peaks, which occurred after the back-to-back recessions of the early 1980s (see Figure 1). In March 2010, 44 percent of unemployed people (a subset of the entire labor force) had been jobless for 27 weeks or more.[6]

A shift away from temporary layoffs and toward permanent layoffs has contributed to the increased duration of unemployment in recent decades. Temporary layoffs, from which a person can reasonably expect to be called back to work, were more common in the recessions of the 1970s and 1980s—when union membership and manufacturing jobs were more prevalent—than in the recessions of the 1 990s and 2000s.[7] If a worker's position is completely eliminated in a permanent layoff, that person must search for and find a new job, probably with a new firm, before heading back to work. That process can take much longer than simply returning to work with a former employer once demand rebounds.

Finding a job may require substantial effort and flexibility, especially when openings are scarce. Some people do not know how to search for a new job effectively. Some find that they need to acquire new skills more suited to the job opportunities available to them or relocate to an area with better prospects. One analysis of data from 1978 to 1990 found that in some states with high rates of unemployment, the unemployment rate decreased only when many of the unemployed people moved to a different state.[8] Even before the most recent recession, a declining share of the population was moving; now, when a significant share of homeowners owe more on their mortgage than their house is worth, many people may not be able to sell their house for enough money to enable them to relocate.[9] Still other people may need to consider alternative employment arrangements, including part-time work or self-employment. People who lost a full-time job during the recessions of the early 1980s, early 1990s, and early 2000s were more likely to be subsequently employed in a part-time job than those who lost their job during periods of stronger economic growth.[10] Finally, many people may need to adjust their expectations regarding the pay they are willing to accept in a new job.

The need to shift from one industry to another to gain a new job is partly responsible for workers' prolonged unemployment. Recessions often accelerate the demise or shrinkage of less efficient and less profitable firms, especially those in declining industries. For example, the steel industry in

Pennsylvania suffered substantial cutbacks during the recessions of the early 1 980s, as the industry adjusted to a long-term reduction in demand for steel in the United States coupled with a reduction in demand associated with the recession.[11] Many workers who had acquired experience and skills specific to the steel industry were hard-pressed to find jobs in other industries. Similarly, if the renewable energy sector expanded over time, some workers in traditional energy sectors (such as coal) would have to retool their skills and perhaps change industries to pursue a job.[12] For those who live in an area in which traditional sources of energy have historically been a primary source of jobs, that transition to a new job in a new industry would probably be especially difficult.

The need to shift from one occupation to another is also partly responsible for prolonged unemployment. Demand for workers performing tasks that can be routinized, such as recordkeeping or repetitive assembly, declined between 1970 and 1998 relative to the demand for workers performing other tasks that are more difficult to routinize, such as legal writing or janitorial services.[13] As a result, some workers in the former set of jobs needed to pursue ways to obtain jobs of the latter type.

Leaving the Labor Force

Most people who lose a job for reasons other than poor performance or misconduct eventually find a new job, but others simply leave the labor force altogether (that is, stop looking for work). Between 1981 and 2003, during recessions as well as periods of economic growth, about 10 percent of people who lost their job left the labor force. [14] Some of those people left only after an extended job search.

Among those who lost a job involuntarily between 1981 and 2003, three groups of workers—women, older people, and less-educated people—were more likely to leave the labor force than were others who lost a job.[15] Particularly for second earners in a household (frequently, married women), spending more time caring for family members or participating in volunteer activities may be preferable alternatives to returning to the paid workforce. People with health problems that make it difficult to work may decide to apply for disability benefits instead. And some older people who lose a job may find retirement to be an affordable alternative to looking for work.

EARNINGSAFTERINVOLUNTARY JOB LOSS

In both the short and the long term, people who lose a job for reasons other than poor performance or misconduct and then find a new job see their earnings decline, on average. Short-term declines in earnings—those in the first few years after a job loss—tend to be larger for people who lose a job during or shortly after a recession. People who lost and then found full-time jobs between 1981 and 1983, 1989 and 1993, and 2001 and 2003 (three periods of subpar economic activity) all experienced relatively large initial declines in earnings as compared with people who lost jobs during periods of stronger economic activity between 1984 and 2000. Those who lost jobs from 2001 through 2003 experienced the largest average decline in earnings—14 percent. The average decline in earnings associated with a job loss in periods of stronger economic activity between 1984 and 2000 varied. For people who lost and then found full-time jobs in the late 1 990s, for instance, declines in earnings were relatively small, between zero and 2 percent. During the other nonrecession years, earnings declines were typically 5 percent to 8 percent.[16]

For people who have acquired a substantial amount of firm-specific knowledge, the loss of a job can be associated with a relatively large decline in earnings in the short term. For people who lost and then found a full-time job between 1981 and 2003, initial declines in earnings were larger in percentage terms for those with longer tenure on the job than for those with shorter tenure.[17] Among men who lost their jobs in a mass layoff during the 1982 recession, older workers (those ages 50 to 55) experienced earnings declines in the year following their job loss that were more than 40 percent higher than the earnings declines of men in their 20s and 30s.[18]

Initial declines in earnings associated with losing a job during a recession may persist for many years. The new job might have both lower earnings and less potential for earnings growth in the future than the lost job.[19] Among the men who lost their job in a mass layoff during the 1982 recession, for example, earnings 15 to 20 years later were about 20 percent lower than those of similar men who did not lose their job. For those who lost their job, earnings declined by about one-third, on average, in the shorter term (a year after job loss).[20] Those estimates include earnings losses for men who did not find a new job (that is, those with no earnings), as well as those who worked full or part time. If the analysis is restricted to men who found a new job after being laid off, the initial and the long-term declines in earnings are smaller but still significant. The long-term losses in earnings for women—at slightly less than 20 percent—were similar to the declines for men. However, women's earnings declined by about 40 percent one year after losing their job in a mass layoff, a larger decline (in percentage terms) than that for men.

Evidence suggests that the long-term decline in earnings associated with a layoff during periods of relatively strong economic growth tended to be smaller than for layoffs during recessions. For men who lost jobs in layoffs at the peak of the late-1980s recovery, the 10-year loss in earnings was about three-fifths as large as for men who lost jobs during the early 1980s recession.[21]

HEALTH INSURANCE COVERAGE AFTER INVOLUNTARY JOB LOSS

Loss of a job often means a loss of health insurance for the worker and perhaps for his or her family. In 2007, before the most recent recession began, over 160 million people under the age of 65—or more than three out of every five nonelderly Americans—had health insurance that was employment based.[22]

During the 1990s, in areas with relatively high unemployment rates, working-age men, whether employed or unemployed, were less likely to have health insurance, but there was no difference in health insurance coverage for working-age women and children.[23] For men under the age of 65, an increase of 1 percentage point in a state's unemployment rate was associated with a decrease of 0.7 percentage points in the probability of having health insurance coverage. No statistically significant relationship between unemployment rates and insurance coverage existed for women and children during that period, in part because Medicaid and, in the late 1990s, the Children's Health Insurance Program provided coverage to families—mostly women and their children—if their income was below certain limits.

No exact counts of the number of people who lost health insurance during the recession that began in December 2007 are available yet. The decline is expected to be substantial, however, because the unemployment rate topped 10 percent in late 2009, and many unemployed people lack health insurance. In the first half of 2009, 33 percent of unemployed adults had been uninsured for more than one year, and an additional 28 percent had been uninsured for at least part of the previous year. As a point of reference, 15 percent of all adults (including unemployed adults) had been uninsured for more than one year, and an additional 10 percent had been uninsured for at least part of the previous year.[24]

Programs That Assist People WhoLose Jobs

A number of government programs are available to help people who have lost their job, such as unemployment insurance (UI) and the Supplemental Nutrition Assistance Program. Disability Insurance (DI) and Supplemental Security Income (SSI) are also available to some people who are unable to work because of a severe health problem. Training and education programs as well as provisions of the Consolidated Omnibus Budget Reconciliation Act of 1985 (COBRA)—which makes possible the continuation of health coverage at group rates for individuals—are also helpful to some people.

Some of the programs are available only to people who have lost their job involuntarily, and others are designed to help people, with or without jobs, who are experiencing misfortune (especially financial distress) for various reasons. The income support or other assistance provided by those programs eases the difficulties often associated with the loss of a job. For some people, however, the availability of support will delay their return to work.[25] A brief description of some of the existing programs appears below, but it is beyond the scope of this brief to elaborate on each program's effectiveness or discuss all relevant programs.

Unemployment Insurance

The UI program targets unemployed people who lose a job for reasons other than poor performance or misconduct. The program is intended to ease labor-market transitions by providing temporary income support to people with sufficient work history who lose their job and are looking for work. Of the 16 million people unemployed in March 2010, 11 million (or about 70 percent) were receiving UI benefits.[26] Because the program temporarily replaces a portion of people's lost earnings, the affected job seekers have less incentive to accept a job offer than they would have otherwise.

The federal government pays states to administer the program, funds benefits for certain groups of unemployed workers, and provides general guidelines and some restrictions on how states may operate their UI programs.[27] Each state sets its own eligibility requirements, determines the duration and amount of regular benefits, and specifies the payroll taxes that fund those programs. In every state, eligibility and benefits are based in part on workers' past earnings, usually from the first four of the previous five completed quarters. The law requires states to screen new UI claimants, identify the ones most likely to exhaust their benefits, and refer them to reemployment services.[28]

The duration of regular UI benefits is generally limited to no more than 26 weeks over a one-year period. In 2009, more than half of the people receiving UI benefits exhausted their regular benefits without finding a job, more than at any time since 1972 (see Figure 2). Many of those workers continued to receive support through the existing extended benefits program or through the emergency unemployment compensation program.

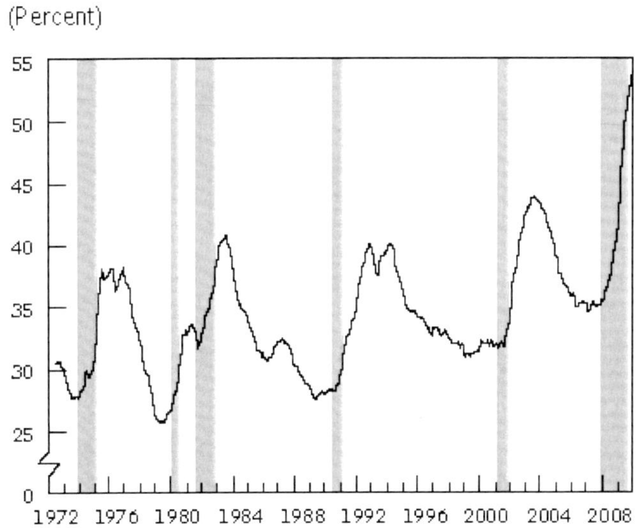

Source: Congressional Budget Office based on data from the Department of Labor, Employment and Training Administration.

Notes: The exhaustion rate is the percentage of unemployment insurance recipients who collect all of the regular benefits to which they are entitled.

The shaded vertical bars indicate the duration of recessions. The National Bureau of Economic Research establishes the dates on which recessions begin and end but has not yet done so for the end of the most recent recession, which is shown as having ended in the second quarter of 2009.

Figure 2. Unemployment Insurance Recipients Who Have Exhausted Their Regular Benefits.

The permanent program for extended benefits provides an additional 13 to 20 weeks of benefits beyond the standard 26 weeks, depending on each state's laws and unemployment rate. That program is usually jointly funded by the federal and state governments, but it is funded completely by the federal government from February 2009 through June 2, 2010 (initially as part of the American Recovery and Reinvestment Act of 2009, or ARRA, and most recently as part of the Continuing Extension Act of 2010). In the week ending March 20, 2010, approximately 200,000 people received benefits through the extended benefits program.[29]

Temporary additional benefits, known as emergency unemployment compensation, are also available in this recession. The current program was established in June 2008 and was most recently extended in April 2010.[30] The program now provides as many as 53 additional weeks of benefits to people who exhaust their other benefits before June 2, 2010. Benefits under the emergency unemployment compensation program are provided in four separate tiers; the first two tiers, of 20 and 14 weeks, are available to people in all states who exhaust their other benefits before June 2, 2010. Benefits for additional tiers of 13 and 6 weeks also may be paid out to people who exhaust the first two tiers, depending on when they exhaust the benefits available to them and whether the unemployment rate in their state reaches certain specified levels.[31] In the week ending March 20, 2010, 5.6 million people received emergency unemployment compensation.[32] Under current law, the program will be closed to new beneficiaries beginning June 2, 2010, and individuals will not be able to qualify for a subsequent tier of benefits after that date.

ARRA (and subsequent extensions) boosted the amount of unemployment benefits that people receive by $25 per week. People who receive any form of unemployment benefits before June 2, 2010, will receive the additional federal compensation. After that date, those beneficiaries will continue to receive the $25 payment until they exhaust whatever form of unemployment compensation they are receiving (regular benefits, extended benefits, or emergency unemployment compensation).

The outlays and revenues of the federal and state programs are recorded in the federal budget. In fiscal year 200 9, outlays for UI benefits totaled $119 billion; about $75 billion of that amount was paid to unemployed workers for benefits under the regular program. Those amounts represent substantial increases over spending for UI in 2007, which totaled $33 billion. Under current law, outlays for UI benefits will total about $156 billion in fiscal year 2010, CBO estimates, of which about $81 billion will be paid to unemployed workers for benefits under the regular program, $7 billion will be used to provide extended benefits, $55 billion will be used to provide emergency unemployment compensation, and $13 billion will cover the added $25 per week in federal compensation. About 15 million workers will begin receiving regular UI benefits in 2010, in CBO's estimation, and they will receive $300 per week for 18 weeks, on average.[33]

Lawmakers are considering legislation that would extend selected UI provisions—emergency unemployment compensation, the full federal funding of extended benefits, and the additional federal compensation—through December 31, 2010.

Supplemental Nutrition Assistance Program

The Supplemental Nutrition Assistance Program, formerly known as the Food Stamp program, provides food assistance to low-income people, including those who have lost a job. Outlays for the program totaled $56 billion in fiscal year 2009. In December 2009, 39 million people living in 18 million households received more than $5 billion in benefits through the program. (During that month, nearly one in eight Americans received benefits.) The average monthly benefit was about $135 per person, or $293 per household. Although the number of participants grew by about 23 percent between December 2008 and December 2009, total costs increased by roughly 44 percent. Costs have increased disproportionately in part because of a boost in benefits included in ARRA. (As a result of that legislation, for example, a household of four receives $80 more per month.)

Programs for People with Disabilities

People who have lost a job and who have severe disabilities and a sufficient work history may be eligible for benefits from the Disability Insurance program, administered by the Social Security Administration.[34] Benefits are based on people's lifetime earnings. People with relatively low earnings (often less-educated people or people who worked intermittently or part-time) receive a larger percentage of their earnings than other DI recipients. After a two-year waiting period, all people who receive DI benefits—regardless of their age—also qualify for Medicare.

When job opportunities become more scarce, either in the entire economy or in particular localities, people with disabilities who lose their job may be more likely to turn to the DI program for support.[35] A study of the 1988– 1992 period found that an increase of 1 percentage point in the unemployment rate led to a 4 percent increase in DI applications and, after one year, a 3 percent increase in new benefit awards.[36] Coinciding with the recession that began in December 2007, DI applications and awards both increased. In the fourth quarter of 2009, roughly 680,000 people applied to the DI program, 31 percent more than in the fourth quarter of 2007. Over the same period, the number of people awarded DI benefits rose by 20 percent. Almost 8 million people received DI disabled-worker benefits in December 2009; average monthly benefits amounted to nearly $1, 100.[37] In fiscal year 2009, disabled workers on Medicare accounted for 17 percent of the Medicare population and received 16 percent of total benefit payments. The average cost of Medicare services for DI beneficiaries in 2009 was about $9,400 per person.[38]

Another program administered by the Social Security Administration, Supplemental Security Income, provides financial support to aged, blind, or disabled adults and children who have limited income and assets. Unlike DI, eligibility for SSI does not depend on previous work history. At the end of 2009, more than 5 million adults with disabilities received SSI benefits; about 700,000 new SSI awards went to disabled adults in 2009, an increase of 23 percent over new awards in 2007. The average regular monthly benefit for disabled adults in the SSI program in December 2009 was just over $475. The number of children who receive SSI benefits also swelled during the most recent recession, rising by about 10 percent (from 1.1 million in 2007 to 1.2 million in 2009).

Smaller Programs

Provisions of COBRA are intended to assist people who face the loss of their health insurance when they lose their job. Under COBRA, a person may continue health insurance coverage through the insurance plan at their former job for up to 18 months.[39] Involuntary job loss for reasons other than gross misconduct qualifies an individual to participate, and family members may also have the right to continued coverage under the group health insurance plan.

The out-of-pocket cost of health insurance purchased under COBRA tends to be three to five times higher than the cost to workers of employment-based health insurance, because people must pay the share of the premium previously paid by their employers.[40] Eligibility for COBRA has been expanded, and premiums have been temporarily reduced, initially as a part of ARRA and most recently as part of the Continuing Extension Act of 2010, by 65 percent for 15 of the 18 months of eligibility for certain qualified individuals. Those lower premiums apply to workers who were involuntarily terminated from their job between September 2008 and May 2010. The federal government is covering the cost of reducing the premiums by providing tax credits to the employers of those workers who choose COBRA coverage. At the time of ARRA's enactment, the staff of the Joint Committee on Taxation estimated that the program would reduce federal revenues in fiscal years 2009 and 2010 by $14.3 billion and $9.2 billion, respectively.[41]

The federal government also funds other programs intended to help people make the transition from one job to another. Those programs include job-search assistance, job referrals, training,[42] and educational assistance provided through Pell grants and subsidized student loans. Educational assistance is available to, but not specifically targeted at, job seekers. A small fraction of workers who lose their job when international competition leads U.S. firms to close is eligible for benefits under the Trade Adjustment Assistance program. In fiscal year 2009, outlays for that program totaled $440 million.

Other types of assistance have been proposed for people making the transition to new jobs. Examples include proposals to help one-stop career centers place more people in jobs or to supplement the earnings of people who take new jobs with lower pay.[43]

This brief was prepared by Molly Dahl and Joyce Manchester of CBO's Health and Human Resources Division. It and other CBO publications are available at the agency's Web site (www.cbo.gov).

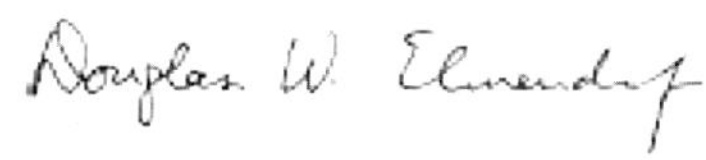

Douglas W. Elmendorf
Director

End Notes

[1] Hereafter, in this brief, the term "involuntary job loss" excludes job loss for poor performance or misconduct.

[2] Recessions examined here include those from November 1973 to March 1975; January 1980 to July 1980; July 1981 to November 1982; July 1990 to March 1991; March 2001 to November 2001; and December 2007 to June 2009. All of those dates but the last one were identified by the National Bureau of Economic Research (NBER); the NBER has not officially determined the end of the last recession, but CBO estimates that it occurred last June.

[3] Congressional Budget Office, *The Budget and Economic Outlook: Fiscal Years 2010 to 2020* (January 2010), Chapter 2.

[4] See Sarah A. Burgard, Jennie E. Brand, and James S. House, "Toward a Better Estimation of the Effect of Job Loss on Health," *Journal of Health and Social Behavior*, vol. 48, no. 4 (December 2007), pp. 369–384.

[5] Congressional Budget Office, *Long-Term Unemployment* (October 2007), Box 2, p. 11. Those estimates are based on survey responses from January 2006 regarding jobs lost in 2003. Some survey participants will probably not recall (and therefore will not report) all jobs lost two years before the survey. And respondents are probably more likely to forget job losses associated with little or no hardship. That is, respondents may be less likely to report job losses associated with relatively short periods of unemployment. See Congressional Budget Office, *Displaced Workers: Trends in the 1980s and Implications for the Future* (February 1993), Figure A-1, p. 44.

[6] Bureau of Labor Statistics, "The Employment Situation—March 2010," news release, USDL-10-0394 (April 2, 2010).

[7] In 1975, 1980, and 1982, about 20 percent of unemployed people were on temporary layoff. In 2009, 11 percent were. See Bureau of Labor Statistics, "Table A-11: Unemployed Persons by Reason for Unemployment," available at www.bls.gov/webapps/ legacy/cpsatab1 1 .htm.

[8] Olivier Jean Blanchard and Lawrence F. Katz, "Regional Evolutions," *Brookings Papers on Economic Activity*, no. 1 (1992), pp. 1–75.

[9] William H. Frey, *The Great American Migration Slowdown: Regional and Metropolitan Dimensions* (Brookings Institution, December 2009); and Congressional Budget Office, *The Budget and Economic Outlook: Fiscal Years 2010 to 2020.*

[10] Henry S. Farber, "What Do We Know About Job Loss in the United States? Evidence from the Displaced Workers Survey, 1984–2004," *Economic Perspectives* (Spring 2005), pp. 13–28.

[11] See General Accounting Office, *The Health of the U.S. Steel Industry*, GAO/NSIAD-89-193 (July 1989), pp. 28–35.

[12] Congressional Budget Office, *The Economic Effects of Legislation to Reduce Greenhouse-Gas Emissions* (September 2009).

[13] See David H. Autor, Richard J. Murnane, and Frank Levy, "The Skill Content of Recent Technological Change: An Empirical Exploration," *Quarterly Journal of Economics*, vol. 118, no. 4 (November 2003), pp. 1279–1333.

[14] See Farber, "What Do We Know About Job Loss in the United States?"

[15] Ibid.

[16] Ibid.

[17] Ibid.

[18] People who lose a job in a mass layoff are a subset of those who involuntarily lose a job more generally. See Till M. von Wachter, Jae Song, and Joyce Manchester, *Long-Term Earnings Losses Due to Mass Layoffs During the 1982 Recession: An Analysis Using U.S. Administrative Data from 1974 to 2004* (working paper, Columbia University, April 2009), available at www.columbia.edu/ ~vw21 12/papers/mass_layoffs_1982.pdf.

[19] Farber, "What Do We Know About Job Loss in the United States?"

[20] Von Wachter, Song, and Manchester, *Long-Term Earnings Losses Due to Mass Layoffs During the 1982 Recession.*

[21] Ibid.

[22] John Holahan and Allison Cook, *Changes in Health Insurance Coverage, 2007–2008: Early Impact of the Recession* (Menlo Park, Calif.: Kaiser Family Foundation Issue Paper, October 2009).

[23] John Cawley and Kosali I. Simon, "Health Insurance Coverage and the Macroeconomy," *Journal of Health Economics,* vol. 24 (2005), pp. 299–3 15.

[24] Michael E. Martinez and Robin A. Cohen, "Health Insurance Coverage: Early Release of Estimates from the National Health Interview Survey, January–June 2009" (National Center for Health Statistics, December 2009), available at www.cdc.gov/ nchs/data/nhis /earlyrelease/insur2009 12.pdf.

[25] For instance, the availability and size of UI benefits may somewhat discourage recipients from accepting less desirable jobs. The effect is probably less pronounced when work is especially hard to find. See Congressional Budget Office, *Options for Responding to Short-Term Economic Weakness* (January 2008), p. 17.

[26] Bureau of Labor Statistics, "The Employment Situation—March 2010," Table A-14; and Department of Labor, "Unemployment Insurance Weekly Claims Report" (April 8, 2010).

[27] For instance, the federal government funds benefits for unemployed federal workers.

[28] See section 4 of the Unemployment Compensation Amendments of 1993 (Public Law 103-152, 107 Stat. 1517); and Stephen A. Wandner, "Employment Programs for Recipients of Unemployment Insurance," *Monthly Labor Review* (October 2008).

[29] Department of Labor, "Unemployment Insurance Weekly Claims Report."

[30] The Supplemental Appropriations Act of 2008 (P.L. 110-252), signed on June 30, 2008, established the program. The most recent extension was part of the Continuing Extension Act of 2010 (P.L. 111-157). States differ in the order in which benefits are taken. In some states, a person must exhaust both his or her regular and extended benefits before receiving emergency benefits. In other states, a person moves from receiving regular benefits to receiving emergency benefits to receiving extended benefits.

[31] The maximum number of weeks a person can possibly receive unemployment benefits is 99. That would include 26 weeks of regular benefits, 20 weeks of extended benefits, and all tiers (20 + 14 + 13 + 6 weeks) of emergency unemployment compensation.

[32] Department of Labor, "Unemployment Insurance Weekly Claims Report."

[33] That benefit amount excludes the additional $25 per week.

[34] Under the rules of the Social Security Administration (SSA), a person is considered disabled if that individual cannot do the work he or she did before or if he or she cannot adjust to other work because of a medical condition (the SSA makes that determination) and if the disability has lasted or is expected to last for at least a year or result in death.

[35] David H. Autor and Mark G. Duggan, "The Growth in the Social Security Disability Rolls: A Fiscal Crisis Unfolding," *Journal of Economic Perspectives*, vol. 20, no. 3 (Summer 2006), pp. 7 1–96.

[36] David C. Stapleton and others, "Introduction," in Kalman Rupp and David C. Stapleton, eds., *Growth in Disability Benefits: Explanations and Policy Implications* (Kalamazoo, Mich.: W.E. Upjohn Institute for Employment Research, 1998), Exhibit 1.2, p. 15.

[37] Data come from the Social Security Administration and are available at www.ssa.gov/OACT/STATS/dibStat.html *and* www.ssa.gov/OACT/STATS/dib-g3.html.

[38] Benefits exclude drug benefits under Part D of Medicare. See Department of Health and Human Services, "2009 CMS Statistics," Tables I.1 and III.5, available at www.cms.hhs.gov/ResearchGenInfo/02_CMSStatistics.asp.

[39] See section 10001 of the Consolidated Omnibus Budget Reconciliation Act of 1985 (P.L. 99-272, 100 Stat. 222).

[40] See Kaiser Family Foundation and Health Research and Educational Trust, *Employer Health Benefits: 2009 Annual Survey* (Menlo Park, Calif., and Chicago, Ill., 2009).

[41] In general, the employer is reimbursed for the portion of the premium not paid by the employee through a credit against its payroll taxes.

[42] See title III of the Workforce Investment Act of 1998 (P.L. 105-220, 112 Stat. 1080).

[43] See Louis S. Jacobson, *Strengthening One-Stop Career Centers: Helping More Unemployed Workers Find Jobs and Build Skills,* Hamilton Project Discussion Paper 2009-01 (Washington, D.C.: Brookings Institution, April 2009); and Gary Burtless, "Income Supports for Workers and Their Families: Earnings Supplements and Health Insurance," in Harry J. Holzer and Demetra Smith Nightingale, eds., *Reshaping the American Workforce in a Changing Economy* (Washington, D.C.: Urban Institute Press, 2007).

Chapter Sources

The following chapters have been previously published:

Chapter 1 – This is an edited, excerpted and augmented edition of a United States Congressional Research Service publication, Report Order Code R44179, dated May 3, 2010.

Chapter 2 – This is an edited, excerpted and augmented edition of a United States Congressional Research Service publication, Report Order Code R40080, dated May 26, 2010.

Chapter 3 – This is an edited, excerpted and augmented edition of a United States Congressional Research Service publication, Report Order Code R40798, dated September 8, 2009.

Chapter 4 –This is an edited, excerpted and augmented edition of a United States Congressional Research Service publication, Report Order Code RL34340, dated March 5, 2009.

Chapter 5 – This is an edited, excerpted and augmented edition of a United States Congressional Research Service publication, Report Order Code R40655, dated June 19, 2009.

Chapter 6 – This is an edited, excerpted and augmented edition of a United States Congressional Research Service publication, Report Order Code R41017, dated January 14, 2010.

Chapter 7 – This is an edited, excerpted and augmented edition of a United States Congressional Research Service publication, Report Order Code R40198, dated November 10, 2009.

Chapter 8 – This is an edited, excerpted and augmented edition of a United States Congressional Research Service publication, Report Order Code R40052, dated December 15, 2008.

Chapter 9 – This is an edited, excerpted and augmented edition of a United StatesCongressional Budget Office publication, dated April 22, 2010.

INDEX

N

O

P

Q

R